MANIFESTING MAGIC

MANIFEST LIKE A WITCH!

ISABELLA JAMES

© Copyright 2022 - All rights reserved.

The content contained within this book may not be reproduced, duplicated or transmitted without direct written permission from the author or the publisher.

Under no circumstances will any blame or legal responsibility be held against the publisher, or author, for any damages, reparation, or monetary loss due to the information contained within this book, either directly or indirectly.

Legal Notice:

This book is copyright protected. It is only for personal use. You cannot amend, distribute, sell, use, quote or paraphrase any part, or the content within this book, without the consent of the author or publisher.

Disclaimer Notice:

Please note the information contained within this document is for educational and entertainment purposes only. All effort has been executed to present accurate, up to date, reliable, complete information. No warranties of any kind are declared or implied. Readers acknowledge that the author is not engaged in the rendering of legal, financial, medical or professional advice. The content within this book has been derived from various sources. Please consult a licensed professional before attempting any techniques outlined in this book.

By reading this document, the reader agrees that under no circumstances is the author responsible for any losses, direct or indirect, that are incurred as a result of the use of the information contained within this document, including, but not limited to, errors, omissions, or inaccuracies.

CONTENTS

Welcome Adventurer   vii

1. WHAT IS MAGIC?   1
   - Magic if You're Not From Hogwarts   1
   - History of Magic and Witchcraft   3
   - Types of Magic and Magical Practitioners   5
   - How is Magic Different From Manifestation?   9

2. MAGICAL SUPPLIES AND TOOLS—GET YOUR INNER WITCH ON!   11
   - Calling a Spade, a Spade—What Are Magical Tools?   11

3. MANIFESTATION TECHNIQUES ON FLEEK   19
   - Manifestation and the Law of Attraction   19
   - Manifestation Techniques   22

4. ENERGY AND MANIFESTATION—NOT JUST FOR HIPPIES   33
   - Why Your Energy Matters   33
   - Frequencies: Not Just For Your Radio   38
   - Raising Your Vibration   40
   - Energy Healing   43

5. MANIFESTATION MAGIC—A LITTLE HOCUS POCUS   45
   - Magical Correspondences   45
   - How to Design Your Own Manifestation Spell   50
   - How to Protect Yourself When Working With Magic   58
   - RESPECT—Find Out What it Means to Me   59

6. HOW TO USE HERBS, ESSENTIAL OILS, AND CRYSTALS TO SUPPORT MANIFESTATION   61
   - Fantastic Herbs and How to Use Them   61
   - Crazy For Crystals   65
   - Essential Oils, Not Just For Your Bath   67
   - How to Make and Use Sigils   68

7. DIVINATION, SCRYING, AND TAROT, OH MY!	71
What is Divination? Can I Tell My Future?	71
Tarot Cards	73
Scrying - Look into My Crystal Ball	81
8. YOUR STATE OF MIND AND SELF-CARE—GLOW UP FOR GREATNESS	83
How Your State of Mind Can Change Your Life	83
What is Self-Care?	85
Ways That You Can Practice Self-Care	88
9. THE POWER OF MEDITATION AND AFFIRMATIONS—YES YOU CAN!	97
Meditation: More Than Just Cross-Legged Oms	97
Meditation Techniques	100
Affirmations: How Do They Work?	103
Affirmations: Where to Start	106
10. SPELLS FOR BEGINNERS—MANIFESTING YOUR DREAM LIFE	109
Spells For Money	109
Spells For Protection	112
Spells For Jobs and Your Career	115
Spells For Love and Relationships	117
Spells For Health and Healing	120
10 Points to Gryffindor	123
Glossary	125
References	127
About the Author	133

This book is dedicated to my children, for they are the most magical creatures on this earth and the light in my life.

WELCOME ADVENTURER

Salutations, and welcome to your journey into the realm of manifestation magic! This guide will assist you to understand the roots of manifestation and how it can be combined with magic to transform your life and attain the power to achieve your goals.

Everyone has suffered with a feeling of powerlessness at some point in their lives. The path to achieving your heart's desires, whether it be related to your career, relationships, money, or personal appearance can sometimes feel like an uphill battle on a very slow horse.

Feeling helpless to change your circumstances is an awful sensation and can even affect your general outlook on life, potentially resulting in despondency and depression. One study even found that such a feeling can cause you to find tasks more difficult and cause objects to appear heavier. Talk about the weight of the world on your shoulders!

The need for control over your life and the ability to achieve your goals is a universal human need. Scientists have found that this is biological in origin, meaning that we are *born* with this need. So what do you do when this need is unmet and you've done everything in your power to achieve your goals without much success?

You take back your control and manifest your goals! A more detailed description of manifestation will be included in later chapters, but manifestation is the act of bringing about your desires through the power of your will and intention.

The purpose of your life is joy. You have the freedom to create the life of your dreams. If you are not experiencing joy, there is a disconnect somewhere in your life; we want to help you fix that! There is no reason why you can't and shouldn't experience a wonderful life filled with so many good and amazing things. We want you to enjoy the journey and revel in the manifestation of everything you've ever wanted.

A way to enhance your manifestation is through magic. Not swish and flick, hocus-pocus magic, but real world magic that is considerably less flashy but still incredibly effective. As with manifestation, a more substantial explanation of magic will be explored in later chapters, but this magic involves effecting changes on the world through your will as well as natural and energetic powers from the natural world.

To benefit from this guide, you don't need to have any prior experience with witchcraft and you don't need a letter from any magical schools. You will also not need to follow a specific religion, faith, or spirituality. This guide is for everyone and anyone who needs to take back the power in their lives and shift their perceptions of the world.

As the focus for this book will be manifestation, we will not be focusing on hexes, jinxes, or mischievous magic, so if you're a prankster looking for new exciting methods, this is unfortunately not the place to find it.

For those of you concerned about the way that this magic will be performed, it will not require the harm of animals, other people, or yourself. No virgins will need to be sacrificed and you won't need any flashy requirements like volcanoes or ancient runes.

For the cash-strapped readers, you will be thrilled to learn that while certain tools and ingredients can assist in enhancing your manifestation, all you really need is your intention and belief.

So, if you're ready, buckle in and get ready for a dive into the depths of manifestation, magic and how to reach the life of your dreams!

1

WHAT IS MAGIC?

So first things first, what is magic and does it involve wands, cauldrons, or unsightly warts on your nose? In this chapter, we will cover what magic means in a non-fictional sense, where it came from, the different types of magic, and what makes magic different from manifestation.

MAGIC IF YOU'RE NOT FROM HOGWARTS

A notable witch and popular writer of witchcraft guides, Scott Cunningham, defines magic as:

"...the projection of natural energies to produce needed effects." (Cunningham, 2004)

Put simply, magic is influencing the world or the outcomes of situations through the application of your will supported by the energy of the natural and spiritual world. Depending on the magic and practitioner, the spiritual aspect may be less or completely absent as practicing magic is a deeply personal activity performed for different reasons.

For some, it is a way of connecting with their deity, for others, it may be a way of connecting with certain spirits (or indeed simply the spirit of the earth) and for the rest, it is just another method of getting things done. Thus, magical power can be divided into the categories of:

- Personal power : the power within yourself (your will and intent.)
- Natural or Earth power: power from the earth and natural elements (fire, water, earth, air.)
- Divine power: power from a deity or spirit.

As witchcraft is a personal journey, practitioners may use one, two, or all of the above categories within their practice.

As you can already see, real world magic is somewhat different from the magic represented in fiction and pop culture. As handy as it would be to wave a wand and turn your ex into a toad or mutter a few words and suddenly look like your favorite celebrity, real magic takes time in addition to having limits. Sadly, you won't be able to bring back loved ones that have passed, reverse or cure chronic or incurable illnesses, make things materialize out of thin air, or instantly turn yourself into royalty.

What you *will* be able to do is manifest positive changes in your life, such as get a specific job, advance your career, promote better communication or intimacy in relationships, or even help increase the money in your bank account. However, these things will not be instantaneous. While there is no hard and fast rule about how long magically manifesting a particular outcome will take; it is a generally held belief that the further away or more 'difficult' the desired outcome, the longer the magic will take.

For example, if you've just started as an intern at a job and you set an intention and do a spell to become the CEO of the company, that's not going to happen the very next day. Likewise, if you are doing a spell to lose 20 lbs, that will manifest quicker than if you set your intention to lose 60 lbs. Additionally, one could try to move their focus away from the "losing weight" aspect and focus on the positive aspects of being healthier.

We'll cover magical correspondences in more detail later in the book but these correspondences are a large part of magic and rituals. Magical correspondences are the energy that certain colors, days of the week, herbs, crystals, and symbols attract or "go with." For example, rose quartz is often known as a "love crystal" because it has energy and emits vibrations that deal with love and relationships (among other things.) You would combine this crystal in a spell or ritual with the colors red or pink and add a herb such as lavender, which also symbolizes love, to manifest an intention to do with love or romantic relationships (whether that is to find a partner, strengthen a relationship, or increase passion.)

The good news is that, unlike in movies and books, you don't need to be chosen or born a certain way to do magic. If you're willing to put in the work and hone the strength of your will and belief, anyone can do magic!

HISTORY OF MAGIC AND WITCHCRAFT

Rituals and what would be considered magic today to bring about certain outcomes are believed to date all the way back to the Stone Age, along with the original deities that sparked the first religions. One of the first recorded examples of this is a clay figure called the Venus of Willendorf found in Austria that dates back to as early as 30,000 BCE. It is believed to be a statue representing an ancient Goddess and was likely used in rituals to promote fertility and abundance.

The cultures of agricultural societies around 10,000 BCE involved practices and rituals that revolved around the seasons and cycles of the natural world. During certain times of the year, they were thought to have performed rituals to encourage a good harvest, protect against drought or disease, or invoke defense for their animals during winter.

As is to be expected, many of these rituals and ceremonies were designed to invoke the power of the earth and the particular deities of the time. Hence, the history of magic goes hand in hand with the development and origins of the earliest Pagan religions.

As societies changed and evolved over time, so too did their deities, each taking on the virtues and unique essence of their civilizations. This, in turn, caused an evolution in the rituals and ceremonies performed. In areas where trade was a primary concern for example, rituals and talismans for abundant trade, good deals, and safe travels became plentiful.

Then came Christianity's rise to power within the prominent Roman Empire in the 4th century. With it came the banning of non-Christian religions and practices. The practice of witchcraft was officially outlawed in the 14th century, charged as heresy, and if convicted, the punishment was death by execution. The long list of practices that constituted witchcraft included herbalism and folk healing commonly performed by healers and midwives. With such strict measures, other magics, rituals, or ceremonies had to be abandoned or practiced in secrecy.

It was only in the 18th and 19th centuries in Europe that an interest in ancient cultures, practices, and religions began to surface. This was greatly aided by the national liberation and romanticist movements that promoted subjectivity, inspiration, and the importance of individuality.

As various nations began to loosen their religious enforcement of mainstream religions, individuals were able to explore their beliefs and spirituality with greater purpose and even form their own religious and spiritual organizations freely. This also allowed scholars to delve more deeply into the histories of religions and cultures pre-Christianity and publish their works without fear of reprisal.

It is only through the painstaking research and subsequent publications of individuals such as Margaret Murray, Gerald Gardner, Aleister Crowley, and several others that we are aware of some of the details of the cultural practices, rituals, and ancient Pagan religions today.

That being said, the rituals and magic that we know today can only be considered an earnest attempt at a revival of the rituals of the past. As with Neo-Paganism, there is a vast divide in the practices today and the magic of antiquity. The considerable gaps in our collective knowledge means that those practicing magic have had to fill in and improvise as best as possible.

TYPES OF MAGIC AND MAGICAL PRACTITIONERS

As you've discovered, the history of magic and witchcraft is vast and spanned many different civilizations. As a result, not only did different religions and deities form, but so too did people discover and develop different types of magic. It is important to note that no type of magic is more or less powerful or valid than any other. The emphasis may be different, but the effectiveness of the magic usually lies in the comfort, intent, and will of the practitioner. We've covered just a few of the different schools of magic below, but there are, in fact, many types that have several of their own subtypes.

Neo-Druidism

Neo-Druidism is a religion and practice that emphasizes a deep reverence for and connection to nature and ancestors while promoting peace and respect for all beings, in addition to holding all knowledge sacred.

As a result, their rituals and magic tend to be earth centric and nature-based. The practices in Neo-Druidism tend to differ according to the individual path and group in question, but usually involve meditation or communing with nature, extensive study of the lore of plant, star, tree, and animal, in addition to engaging in philosophical musings. Rituals and divination may also be performed to encourage certain outcomes, such as rain in a drought or peace in war time. Depending on the beliefs of the individual, prayers may also play a part within their faith and magical practices.

Neo-Shamanism

Neo-Shamanism is a practice and way of life that uses certain techniques to experience alternative realities through a purposeful shift of consciousness to heal illnesses physical, mental, and spiritual, communicate with the spirits and entities within other planes for guidance and learning, and to conduct the souls of the dead to the otherworld. This altered state of consciousness can be achieved through drumming, dancing, chanting, exposure to the elements (extreme heat or cold), fasting, or mind-altering substances.

Most, if not all, shamanistic magic is performed through a state of trance and is usually performed to manifest positive outcomes for those close to them or their community. Being a shaman is usually considered to be a duty, and thus their magic is not usually used to manifest outcomes that they personally desire.

Ceremonial Magic

Ceremonial magic is exactly what it sounds like: magic

performed through ceremony. It is magic performed within a designed ritual, in a sacred or cleansed space, usually with a multitude of accessories to aid the outcome of the ritual. What many witches call a 'circle' is a good example of ceremonial magic and usually serves as the basis for the casting of particular rituals.

A magical circle is a sacred space, cleansed of harmful energy and encircled by an actual circle of salt, chalk, egg shells, or a visualized circle. This is used as an area that protects and amplifies magical rituals. Chanting in verse, ceremonial items such as a chalice, or the representation of the elements are common for ceremonial magic.

This type of magic can assist in raising energy for certain rituals as it may include dancing, drumming or singing, and can be done individually or in a group. Ceremonial magic is a common form of magic done when multiple individuals are involved and is a good way to combine energies toward a singular purpose.

Folk and Natural Magic

Folk magic is practical magic used to solve the problems of daily life. Healing, attracting love, bringing luck, money, or providing protection from people or spirits are common examples of the type of problems this type of magic usually solves.

The specific methods of the magic itself is usually particular to the area or region that the practitioners are in, as various countries have their own rituals and practices. Some examples of practices that may be more popular in some geographical areas than others include the use of poppets (like a voodoo doll), muti (traditional medicine in Africa), or hex signs (symbols used to protect areas.)

However, as the world has become more connected and

people have shared their techniques and experiences with others, folk magic methods have increasingly become the personal choice of the practitioner. Folk magic may also include the creation of talismans, inscriptions, and the use of knot magic.

Natural or 'nature' magic, as the name suggests, involves the use of natural elements to work one's will. This type of magic encompasses a few sub genres of magic, including herbal magic, crystal magic, elemental magic, kitchen magic, astrology, weather magic, lunar and solar-based magic, and any other magic that uses natural elements as its base.

Divination

Divination is a form of magic that serves for practitioners to gain insight or guidance for specific situations. Magical methods of divination include but are not limited to the tarot, rune magic, oomancy (egg readings), tea leaf readings, ceromancy (candle wax readings), lithomancy (stone readings), aeromancy (weather reading), and to a degree, dowsing magic among many others.

Hexes, Jinxes, and Curses

These are generally considered to be the more 'taboo' or darker magics as they actively seek to negatively impact other people.

There is some debate on what sets the three apart, but it is generally believed that jinxes are short term malicious magics that result in poor luck and small misfortunates but aren't intended to cause severe harm (no major illness, deaths, or considerable losses.)

Hexes are a longer lived, more powerful form of hostile

magic that is often meant to teach the victim a lesson, after which, the hex will be broken.

The most powerful form of malignant magic is the curse. It can cause severe consequences that can haunt and cripple the victim in multiple ways and may last a lifetime or even well into their children's generations and further.

Some practitioners believe that performing these magics may well result in the caster experiencing misfortune due to karma or a high likelihood of the magic backfiring. Others believe that they should have the power to get revenge or hurt those that have wronged them, and with proper protection, casters should suffer no ill-effects. This is a hotly debated topic within magical communities and greatly depends on the specific path chosen by the individual.

As you can see, there are a plethora of different magics and associated paths and, in fact, there are actually many more than what was mentioned above. Some practitioners follow a strict path and only use specific magical methods, while others tend to mix and match according to what suits them. Either way is correct, as witchcraft and magic are deeply personal journeys with no two being the same.

HOW IS MAGIC DIFFERENT FROM MANIFESTATION?

So if magic is using your will and intention to manifest a certain outcome, how is it different from manifestation? While having similar elements, magic also usually calls on the power of the earth, natural energies, deities, and spirits to enhance and assist with working your will.

Most practitioners of magic also work closely with the aforementioned correspondences, doing spells at certain times of the lunar or solar cycle, or making use of herbs, crystals, and the like. For many, magic is a spiritual and/or religious calling, so their workings often have a greater depth and level of seriousness to them than standard manifestation, as it is their way of connecting with their deity, the earth, or the spiritual world.

However, if your spells simply involve invoking your personal power to manifest your will without any of this, then it certainly can be called manifestation as opposed to magic.

Ultimately manifestation is a large part of practicing magic, so whether you view it as very separate or one and the same, the most important factor is that it works for you.

2

MAGICAL SUPPLIES AND TOOLS—GET YOUR INNER WITCH ON!

Now that you know a little bit more about what magic is and the different kinds out there, you must be wondering what you'll need to start. The great news is that you don't actually *need* anything to perform magic. The power is within you at all times, so all you have to do is use it (use the force!). But sometimes, magical tools and supplies help you to strengthen your magic in addition to giving you a focus. So let's jump into our magical bag and see what kind of tools you could use.

CALLING A SPADE, A SPADE—WHAT ARE MAGICAL TOOLS?

First of all, what makes a tool magical and what are they used for? Unlike in various fantasy lands where your magical items of choice choose you and are imbued with all sorts of fantastic properties, magical tools and supplies are merely items that you use within your magical workings. (As much as we all want a ring that makes you invisible or a cupboard to another world.)

What makes these items magical is your intent and the way that you use them. Some individuals go as far as to make all their tools from scratch to imbue it with their personal energy and theoretically boost their power. Buying items you use in your rituals doesn't make the magic any less powerful, however, it's all to do with what works for you (magic has major "you do you, boo" vibes.)

This also applies to what specific tools are in any magic user's arsenal. Some only feel they need one or two tools, while others feel they need different tools for different purposes, and yet others feel that they need no tools at all.

It is important to note that, when working any kind of magic, it is common for witches to cleanse their tools before and after using them to ensure that no lingering energy has any unintended effects on their current or future spells.

The Besom (or Broom)

The besom, or broom, is a common magical tool often used to cleanse an area of negative energy or to rid the area of residual energy after a spell. Traditionally, the besom has been used within protection and purification rituals. For example, laying a broom across the threshold of a house prevents negative spells from entering, protecting the residents, while sleeping with a broom under the pillow is believed to protect the sleeper from nightmares and psychic attacks.

It is also sometimes considered to represent the sacred sexual union between the God and Goddess, or universal masculine and feminine energies, with the bristles portraying the women's genitals and the handle representing the phalus. Thus, it has also been used within love and intimacy magic. In addition, it has been known to form a traditional part of handfastings (pagan weddings.) Couples would jump over a broom to formalize their union.

If you want a besom of your very own, you can go the whole hog of making it yourself by carving or finding a wooden branch to create the staff and attaching bristles with some kind of binding. Traditionally, this would be an ash staff for protection, willow binding for feminine energy, and birch bristles, which are purifying, but you are welcome to use whatever ingredient you have available or calls to you specifically.

There is also nothing wrong with buying a broom and then dedicating it to your magical practice. You can add gemstones or ribbons to it, or decorate it in a way that speaks to you, or simply smudge it with sage (pass it through the smoke of burning sage) or leave it in moonlight overnight to cleanse it.

Thereafter, simply dedicate it to your magic practices. It is important to note that one shouldn't use such a tool to sweep the floor of dirt or for mundane purposes (no smacking creepy crawlies with it!). Once you have dedicated a tool to your practice, it must only be used for magical workings and should be treated with respect.

The Athame and Boline (Ritual Knives)

Before you panic, both types of ritual knives in magic practice are not meant to cut into people or animals, or used in any kind of ritual sacrifice.

To start, an athame (often pronounced atha-may), is a double-edged knife with a black handle. The double edge is often meant to represent duality (masculine and feminine, spiritual and mundane.) This knife is used for directing and cutting energy. At no time is it used to cut actual physical things (please don't cut your vegetables with it.) As a result, many practitioners prefer for it to be a blunt knife, but there aren't any rules about it.

It can be used to cast your circle by drawing it on the ground around you, used for cord-cutting rituals (cutting your spiritual ties to undesirable places, people, or things), or for directing your will in a ritual (a bit like a wand.) It is also believed that the handle stores residual power that is raised during rituals for later use.

A boline, by contrast, is a white-handled knife that is usually slightly sharper by merit of it being for more practical uses. This is the knife that is used to cut herbs and wood (for magical uses, not for cooking), carve runes into talismans, candles, or the like, and cut ropes or cord for certain rituals. While this knife is more practical, it also should not be used for mundane practices such as gardening, chopping food, or getting lint from under your nails. Like other magical tools, it should be dedicated as such and treated with respect.

As most people don't have the skill or know-how to make their own knives from scratch, most magic users tend to buy them. If you have a magical supply store, you may find some made exactly for such a purpose but if that is not available to you, a regular kitchen knife will do. Feel free to decorate your knives in any way that calls to you. To cleanse your knives before using them, you can plunge them into the earth for 12 hours or store them in a bowl of salt for the same amount of time.

Cauldron: Double, Double, Toil, and Trouble!

The cauldron is probably one of the most iconic symbols of witchcraft, going all the way back to Shakespeare's representation of the three witches over the bubbling pot.

A cauldron is traditionally a cast-iron, three-legged pot with a handle. They come in a variety of sizes, from the large ones you see in fictional films and series, to small, portable versions the size of a large mug.

As far as magical workings go, the use of cauldrons are quite diverse. They are traditionally associated with feminine energy, water, creation, transformations, fertility, and the element of water. Some witches may use the cauldron for creating potions, while others use it as a receptacle in which to ritually burn items, create a safe space for a ritual flame, or fill it with magically charged water to drink, scry, or to consecrate a space with. Some magic users, for practical reasons, prefer to conduct edible magical workings within a standard pot on a stove as opposed to in a cauldron on an open fire. As before, the intent and belief provide the power to your workings; the tools just assist you to focus it.

Cleansing a cauldron can be done with soapy water first and then left in the moonlight overnight. Be sure that any residual herbs, ash, or other components have been thoroughly cleaned out before starting a new ritual. Anything used that can spoil may rot, which is not a smell you want to deal with!

Finding your own cauldron may be challenging or easy depending on where you live. Most magical supply stores will stock cauldrons, but if you are struggling to find one, a cast iron pot will also do just fine.

Censor (or Incense Burner)

A censor is simply an incense burner. It can be a simple wooden holder for stick incense, a holder that allows for the burning of coals, or those large complicated singing incense holders that are sometimes seen in Christian churches.

Incense, like with other natural elements, have their own correspondences so they are commonly used in magic rituals. Incense and their censors are considered representative of the element of air. Incense is also often used to cleanse items by passing the items through their smoke.

If you can't find or afford your own incense burner, you can make one with a shell, or bowl with salt or sand. The salt or sand works to absorb the heat so that the bowl does not crack. Incense burners are widely available from many different stores, so you will not need to rely on magical suppliers for this particular tool.

If you have pets, especially cats, please do be careful when using incense indoors as animals tend to be very sensitive to scents and some incense and essential oils can be toxic to them even when just inhaling it. Ensure that when you burn incense with pets in the house that the house is well ventilated and preferably that they can go outside to get away from the scent if it becomes too overwhelming for them.

Wand: Not Like in the Stories

This kind of wand is unfortunately not like the powerful artifact from fictional worlds, items like Gandalf's staff, the White Queen's wand, or even the wands from Harry Potter for that matter. Wands in reality have no more power than you do. They are used to direct your energy and can be used to invoke deities or spirits, draw symbols in the air or on the ground, create your circle, or even to stir magical mixtures in a cauldron.

Traditionally, wands were made of wood and cut from oak, apple, cherry, peach, elder, willow, and other trees, usually by the practitioners themselves. Wand sizes vary greatly, some preferring their wands to be as long as their forearm, while others look for something a little more compact. Magic users in modern times can have wands made from silver, bronze, gemstones, metal, and other types of materials. One can also inscribe sigils or symbols on the wand or adorn them with stones or gemstones.

As with most other tools, you can buy your wand from a magical supply shop, or you can make one yourself. It is usually best to create a wand from dead wood, but if you need to pull a branch from a live tree, be sure to thank the tree and try not to damage it too much in the process.

Chalice (Fancy Cup)

The chalice is, for all intents and purposes, a fancy cup. It represents water and the feminine aspect and is often used to either represent water on the altar, in the ritual, or it is used to hold the ritual drink (this is usually a mixture of water and herbs, teas, or wine and not the blood of innocents; please don't use your chalice like this.)

The chalice can be made of any material that works for you; silver, wood, bronze, pewter, glass (be careful of breakage), or if you've got Scrooge McDuck kind of money, then even a golden one. The material that the chalice is made out of is more to do with personal preference and practical aspects than any mystical ones. Silver, wood, and any kind of metal are less likely to be damaged than glass, ceramic, or clay, and sometimes the choice is that simple.

As with other tools, it can be adorned with crystals or decorations according to the individual's spirituality, religion, or personal aesthetic preference.

Crystal Sphere: Yes, the Magical Crystal Ball

The crystal sphere was used for divination and scrying practices where the practitioner would look for images or insight in the surface, which would provide guidance or insight.

These days, genuine crystal balls are extremely expensive, so many magic users use glass, plastic, or leaded glass balls. All work as effectively as the other, so don't feel pressured to buy the most expensive one you can find.

If you do decide to add this one in your arsenal of witchy things, remember to keep it covered with a cloth at all times, as sadly, several accidents have occured where the sphere acts like a magnifying glass and causes fires (and you thought it would be some mystical reason, didn't you?).

3

MANIFESTATION TECHNIQUES ON FLEEK

All aboard the manifestation train! It's time to get ready for the first step in your journey to achieving your dream life. We'll explore what manifestation is, why it is believed to work both psychologically and energetically, and in addition, you'll get a whole bunch of quick and useful manifestation techniques that you can get started with right away.

MANIFESTATION AND THE LAW OF ATTRACTION

To begin with, what is the law of attraction, and how does it relate to manifestation? The law of attraction is actually a core principle within manifestation as it suggests that a positive mindset brings positive situations and luck into a person's life while a negative mindset attracts undesirable situations and occurrences. This philosophy actually has three core laws or central principles that encompass this belief:

Like attracts like

This means that people with specific mindsets, as well as energy, tend to attract one another like magnets. For example, have you ever noticed that people that love to complain always manage to find each other? The old adage "Misery loves company" certainly applies here. Not only do these people tend to form groups where they feed off each other's negative energy, but from an outside perspective, they also seem as if they have extraordinarily bad luck. Likewise, positive attitudes tend to attract other people with positive attitudes. Think about those people that often seem to breeze through life, avert disaster, and always land on their feet regardless of the situation. Basically, positive attitudes also attract positive results and vice versa.

Nature abhors a vacuum

This law essentially means that it is not possible to have a completely empty space in your life or mind. So by getting rid of negative things, thoughts, and mindsets in your life, you are making way for the positive aspects of those things to come flooding in. Just like you can't pack new clothes into a cupboard that is filled with old, torn clothes, so you also need to make space in your mind and life for the new, exciting manifestations of your dreams by removing those things that no longer serve you, whether it is negative thoughts, people who break you down, or a job that makes you unhappy. One caveat to this is not to just indiscriminately start cutting things out of your life willy-nilly; a bad relationship can be repaired with effort, you don't need to immediately cut that person out of your life, and if you have a job that makes you unhappy, look for a replacement first and secure one; don't just quit and leave yourself without an income.

The present is always perfect

This law means that one should always try to, firstly, be present in the moment, and secondly, try to make the present as positive as possible. This law suggests that you can improve on the present moment with thoughts, words, actions, or simply a good mindset and actively try to see the positive in the situation instead of fixating on the negative. It's important to note here that this does not mean that you need to repress or chastise yourself for feeling negative emotions. Negative emotions are natural, especially in response to stressful or sad situations, and feeling those emotions is an important part of the healing process. What it does mean is that you do what you can to improve the situation or help yourself to feel better and let the rest go.

So how does this work on a psychological level? Studies have demonstrated that those with an optimistic outlook tend to be more creative, productive, better at problem-solving, and better at recognizing as well as taking advantage of opportunities than those with more pessimistic outlooks.

Additionally, the power of the belief in your ability to manifest the things that you want in your life helps you to conquer doubt and boost your confidence, which in turn increases your chance of success in your endeavors. Not only this, but our actions tend to be led by our focus, and when you continuously visualize and focus on working toward a particular goal, this both consciously and subconsciously changes our behavior to work toward achieving this goal.

MANIFESTATION TECHNIQUES

Vision Board

Creating a vision board means solidifying your goals, getting them down in a list and then imagining what those goals would visually look like. Do you want a castle in Scotland? Do you want to be the CEO of your company? What does your dream body look like? Do you want to start a cat cafe? What words would you like people to use to describe you? Once you've solidified your goals and how they look, find images and words that encapsulate your dreams and stick them up on a board that you will see every day. Maybe for you it's your cupboard door or your bedroom mirror, or maybe it's even on your fridge. As long as you know that you can't help but to lay eyes on it, this will help keep your goals clear in your mind and help motivate you to keep working towards them.

Gratitude Journal

A great way to encourage and maintain that optimistic attitude that we're trying to enforce with the first law of attraction (like attracts like) is to keep a gratitude journal. This aids you in feeling grateful for all the good things presently in your life and helps to prevent you from becoming despondent if the things that you are manifesting are taking a bit of time. Constantly thinking about the things that we lack can cause us to forget about and under appreciate the things that we already have. Making a list of the things you are grateful for every morning or night is a great way to start and/or end your day on a good note. Challenge yourself to make a goal of choosing at least 10 items daily that you are grateful for. You will quickly be able to see that there really is a lot to be grateful for in our lives that we often don't even give a second thought. This can include things like having a roof over your head, electricity, running water, or the Internet. Blessings start to become abundant when we look for them.

Meditation Manifestation

Meditation is not only a great way to slow down and truly be in the present, but it can also help you manifest your desires in several different ways. If you are unsure of exactly what you want to manifest or how, such as, if you are unhappy in your life and want to fix it but aren't sure why you're unhappy or what needs to change, meditation can help clear your mind sufficiently to think on this more clearly and get an answer. If you are clear on what it is you want to manifest, meditating on this can help cement this particular goal and its direction in your subconscious. To help you along, you'll find a link to a meditation specifically made for you at the back of this book!

Positive Affirmations

One of the most popular and well-known manifestation techniques, positive affirmations are stating (affirming) positive statements that relate to your goals. For example, "I am successful, I am becoming the CEO, I am constantly improving, I am attaining my dream body." These affirmations can assist you in boosting your confidence and convincing yourself both on a conscious and subconscious level that your goals are within your grasp. It effectively retrains your brain to stop using negative self-talk and self-deprecating statements, which is an all too common habit in today's society.

Saying these affirmations out loud once or several times a day and writing them on a surface that you know you'll see everyday is a great way to start this manifestation practice. To help you, we have created some printable affirmations and you can find the link to these at the end of this book.

Intention Journal

This technique is a good way to formalize your goals and break them into achievable smaller steps. You can use an intention journal to write a list of your broader goals to keep in mind such as getting your dream job or finding your soulmate, but it is also a great way to write your intentions for the day, week, or month for actions to achieve that goal. For example, you could write, "I intend to write 1000 words of my book this week," or, "I intend to meet and speak to three new people this month," or, "I intend to work 2 extra hours of overtime today." If you're more into the digital format, you can use your notes on your phone or even set it as part of a special to-do list. Make it your own!

Scripting Manifestation Techniques

Another of the more well-known manifestation techniques made popular by social media, scripting involves writing down your manifestation like a story, positioning it as if you had already achieved your goals and were writing down how it happened, what you achieved, and how you felt when achieving all these goals. Think it almost as if you're writing the journal of your future self that has already manifested everything that you wanted from life. This helps to cement this as an inevitability in your mind that you will achieve your goals and adds to feelings of confidence and excitement that your dream will be achieved.

55 x 5 Method

Just as writing things down helps you to remember them when studying for tests, writing down your affirmations repeatedly will also help with your manifestation. In order to use this method, all you need to do is turn your goals into affirmations (I will get that promotion), and then write that affirmation down 55 times for 5 consecutive days. As 55 times is a lot of writing, it's usually better to try to be as concise as possible with your affirmation and ensure it is as specific as possible. While writing this affirmation down, hold the goal that you want to achieve in your mind and write with purpose; try not to do it absentmindedly as your focus is important when doing this exercise.

Belief Assessment

Our subconscious can be a crazy place full of contradictions. This is why it is important to perform a belief assessment, as sometimes, our goals don't necessarily align with our beliefs about those goals. For example, if you are trying to manifest a promotion, but deep down you either don't feel like you really deserve it or are afraid that you won't be able to actually handle it, should it come to pass, you will need to get down to the bottom of these limiting beliefs. To do this, reflect carefully on your goal and any potential limiting thoughts you may have about it. Then create some affirmations that link to these negative thoughts ("I do deserve this," or, "I will be able to handle it") and repeat this several times each day.

Two Cup Method

This particular manifestation method will feel a little like a magical ritual. What you'll need is two identical cups of any type, paper, pens, tape/prestik, and water. Label one cup with your current undesirable situation (lonely, unappreciated, broke etc.) and the other cup with the situation you want to manifest (in a loving relationship, enough money to cover bills etc.) and then fill the cup labeled with your current situation with water. Then slowly pour the water from the current situation cup into the manifestation cup while imagining your situation changing, how it might happen and how you will feel when it does. Mindfully drink the water from the manifestation cup. Then remove the label from the current situation cup and throw it away. Keep the label for the manifestation cup in a place where you can see it daily to remind yourself of the situation that you are manifesting for yourself.

Bedtime Reprogramming

If you've heard of people listening to recordings or podcasts of information that they need to learn for a test or presentation while they fall asleep, this manifestation technique works in a similar way. Our subconscious mind can be very influential in directing our waking thoughts and behaviors. One method of influencing our subconscious is through taking advantage of the window between waking and sleep when our subconscious is more likely to take in more information. To use this technique, simply record yourself saying your affirmations or goals out loud and play this recording every night as you go to sleep. This will also help to slowly transition our subconscious away from any limiting beliefs to more positive ones.

Permission Practice

Sometimes, we limit ourselves because at some point in our lives, we've come to believe that we can only achieve the things that we want when we have permission to do so. Whether our belief is that this permission needs to come from a superior, a parent, mentor, or someone else, we need to examine these thoughts and reaffirm that the only people that we need permission from to succeed is ourselves. Sometimes, writing or saying out loud who we believed we needed permission from (and why if you know why) and then renouncing that belief repeatedly, will assist in this practice. Actively giving yourself permission daily will also help in cementing the fact that *only* you are in charge of your success.

Worry Box

Worrying is a very natural and common activity that everyone does from time to time, but sometimes, these worries and anxiety can stand in the way of our manifestations and goals. A great way to rid your mind of these kinds of thoughts is to write them all down on a piece of paper regularly and then either mindfully throw them away, or if you can do so safely, burn them. If you do decide to burn your paper, please do so in a controlled environment and keep a fire extinguisher or hose nearby if you're making a fire to throw it into. When getting rid of these pieces of paper, imagine your worries disappearing from your mind.

Positive Environments

Coming back to the first law of attraction (like attracts like), this means that we have to be more mindful of the people and environments that we surround ourselves with.

This doesn't mean that we have to cut ties with friends or family that don't necessarily fit our goals, but it means that we should actively try to ensure that our environment and people that we engage with are positively aligned with our goals and life that we want to manifest where possible. That being said, it is also important not to become obsessive about this point, as no place or set of people are going to be "optimally aligned" at all times, and trying to be overly controlling of this aspect will cause unnecessary stress and anxiety.

Fake it Till You Make it

This technique is often misinterpreted as "behave like someone else," which in all honesty will not get you far. What this really means is behave the way that your future self would behave had you already manifested your goal. For example, if you want to have a particular position in your company, act confident in meetings, dress for someone in that position, ask questions where necessary, and put in the work that someone of that position would. This relates once again to the first law of attraction, "like attracts like," but also works towards others seeing you the way that you'd like to be seen. If your superiors see you acting the part, the more likely they will be to think that you will be a good fit for your desired position.

Embrace Your Inner Child

Our inner child is the part of us that is the most vulnerable. It retains some of our most firmly held beliefs that were developed in our formative years. Vulnerabilities and beliefs from our inner child may become roadblocks on our journey to manifesting our desires. Healing past wounds and traumas and addressing these vulnerabilities of your inner child may be something that you can do on your own, or you may require the help of a therapist to do this. Doing so may be a powerful step to removing the most stubborn of limitations to achieving our goals and truly manifesting our desires.

Higher Self-Visualization

This is a lovely technique that helps you to get a better picture of your "higher self," that is, what you would look, feel, and act like once you have manifested the life that you dream of. This visualization may just involve closing your eyes, but you can also go into a meditative state if you would prefer this. Imagine what the "ideal you" would look like; how would they sound and carry themselves, where do they work, what does their home look like, who do they surround themselves with, how do they treat others? Then try to keep this image in your mind as you go through your day and actively aspire to be your higher self in any way you can. Bit by bit, if you continue to do this, you can expect your actions to start to align with those of your higher self and thereby manifest the life that comes with it.

Be Like Elsa and Let it Go!

Sometimes, the pressure that we place upon ourselves to manifest everything we want and become a certain person with a specific life can become overwhelming and cause anxiety (sounds like a familiar princess with ice-powers, doesn't it?). When this happens, it is important for you to give yourself permission to let go of these goals and intense focus for a short time and give yourself the space to recharge and rest. This is not forever, and you will want to pick up those manifestation techniques and your focus once again in the future, but sometimes, giving yourself this break is more conducive to achieving your goals than driving yourself too hard.

Start Small

For those new to manifestation that may be harboring doubts (which in turn will hamper your ability to manifest), sometimes it might be helpful to try to start with manifesting something small. Try to manifest something like a free meal or finding $20, and once you have manifested something small, you will build confidence in the practice which will allow you to manifest bigger things more in line with your larger goals. Your belief and confidence in your ability to manifest things that you want directly correlate with your success in doing so.

Pillow Method

Similar to bedtime reprogramming, the pillow method focuses on directing your thoughts right before bed. To use this technique, write your goals or affirmations on a piece of paper right before bed and place it under your pillow. Focusing your thoughts on your goals as the last thoughts you make before you go to sleep will help it filter through to your subconscious, thereby altering your actions towards this focus. Placing it under your pillow doesn't do anything specific, but being able to reread them in the morning is a nice way to reaffirm your goals before you start your day.

369 Method

Similar to the 55 x 5 method, this technique is also great for those that find repetition helpful. To use this method, write down or say aloud the goals that you want to manifest, three times in the morning, six times during the day, and nine times in the evening. Some believe that this should be done for 33 or 45 consecutive days, but how long or short you want this exercise to be is completely up to you. The famous inventor and futurist Nikola Tesla believed that these three numbers are divine (in the special, blessed sense rather than the tasty sense.) He was said to have stated that these numbers could even be part of the key to the universe's secrets. Whether you believe this yourself or not, this technique will certainly help to affirm your goals and keep them at the forefront of your mind throughout the day.

I Remember When Method

This is a fun and whimsical exercise that can assist you in nudging your subconscious mind in the right direction. All you need to do is say or write down, "I remember when..." and then follow that with the goals you want to manifest. The key to this exercise is to pretend that you have already manifested the goal. Think about how it was achieved, what did you do, how did you feel, how long did it take? The more detail that you put into it, the better! This will help you subconsciously change your actions to that of a person that would achieve these goals and will make it easier for you to manifest.

Be Curious; Seek Adventure!

While not a specific technique, this is an important part of getting in the right mindset of manifesting the life of your dreams. While having a comfort zone is fine and sometimes necessary, taking a step outside of what you know is the only way to effect change. Having a different viewpoint will also help you to find out what other goals there might be out there to manifest. Sometimes, our goals that we want to manifest are a little vague, even to us. We want to be interesting, or useful, or successful, but in what way? Sometimes, exploring new interests will help you with this. If you have an attraction to all things arty, try it out. If you are curious about woodwork, or working with your hands, look at some online videos and learn more about it. You may find another side of yourself that will help you enhance the vision of your dream life and give you more direction when thinking of the things that you want to manifest.

Congratulations Technique

Similar to the "I Remember When" method, the congratulations technique involves imagining your family, friends, and loved ones congratulating you on achieving your goals. You can imagine the words that they will use to describe you, the look on their faces when they do so, and even what you believe that you might do to celebrate. Once again, not only does this belief seep into your subconscious, convincing it that this is entirely possible and move your actions towards your focus, but it helps to get you excited about the inevitable future when you do manifest your goals and make your dreams come true.

4

ENERGY AND MANIFESTATION— NOT JUST FOR HIPPIES

It's all about the energy, dude. As it turns out, the hippies were right all along. Not only is energy important in daily life, but it is paramount when it comes to manifestation too. In this chapter, we're going to explore why energy actually matters, what the deal is with frequencies, why and how to raise your vibrations, and the secrets behind energy healing.

WHY YOUR ENERGY MATTERS

To begin with, what is your energy anyway? (Besides what you run out of when you don't get enough coffee.) Your personal energy encompasses a range of things on multiple levels. It includes your thoughts, your beliefs, your values, the way you interact with others, your memories, your emotions, and yes, the 'battery' and motivation required for you to both mentally and physically perform tasks. In fact, you and *everything* around you is made up of energy! Additionally, our energy has the power to affect the energy around us, including the personal energy of others.

As your personal energy encompasses so many areas of

what makes you who you are, it can be broken up into the following categories:

- Physical energy - the energy required to live and physically perform tasks.
- Mental energy - the energy that is required to think, use logic, and make decisions.
- Emotional energy - the energy required to identify, manage, and understand your emotions and that of others.
- Spiritual energy - the energy that you put out into the universe that drives your beliefs, conscience, and values.

Despite being broken into different categories, all these types of energy affect the others. If, for example, you are low on emotional energy, this may impact your physical energy, as it may remove the motivation, if not the physical energy, to do things. There is a constant interplay between your energies, and when any of them are out of balance, it will negatively impact your life, as well as your ability to manifest the things that you want.

So how can we balance our energies, and how are things different when our energies are balanced?

Some ways to manage and take control of your energy are:

Get to know yourself and your needs

Find out what is draining your energy, and what gives you energy. Then explore how to bring more activities and people into your life that provide that positive juju while reducing your exposure (or cutting out) those that drain you.

Become more aware

Sometimes, we are being affected by a person, place, or situation's energy and we're not even aware of it. Ever been into a room when two people have been fighting? That atmosphere affects your energy! Try to notice when an energy shift occurs and pinpoint what the cause of the shift was and whether it is something that is affecting your energy positively or negatively.

Protect yourself

Do your best, where possible, to protect yourself from negative energies. This can be by removing yourself from certain situations, avoiding certain people, or changing your environment to suit your needs. Where it cannot be avoided, take steps to use coping mechanisms to make the effect on you less. If for example, you can't avoid your colleague from making snorting noises, put on some headphones, or if you can't change the atmosphere at home, take walks to get some fresh air and get away from it where possible.

Self-care is important

Self-care can be considered activities that "recharge your batteries" and replenish your energy. These activities can be different for everyone, but might include exercise, meditation, reading, praying, hobbies, or anything else that brings you joy and helps you feel refreshed, rejuvenated, and ready to take on the world. These are the activities that are especially important in cases when you will have repeated exposure to a negative drain on your energy that you currently can't do anything about. This is also how you can prevent yourself from throwing your stapler at Steve when he makes another joke about women belonging in the kitchen.

Try to find coping methods in the moment to rebalance your energy

When it is not possible to engage in a long-duration self-care activity like exercise or meditation, it is important to find ways to manage your energy in the moment and help regain your equilibrium. For example, if you are physically drained, a cup of coffee or a snack may help bring up your energy levels. Likewise, if you are feeling mentally drained, take a break, read something that interests you, or just step outside for some fresh air. You can recover from emotionally draining activities through reading jokes, speaking to loved ones, listening to uplifting music, or turning on a favorite podcast.

Determine if you have any imbalances

Sometimes, your energy levels may be out of balance because you are neglecting a part of yourself. If you neglect your physical energy by not eating right, not sleeping enough, or drinking enough water for example, you will not be able to physically perform tasks as well and may even fall ill. If you neglect your emotional energy through too much or little social interaction or acknowledging your emotions, you may feel lonely, anxious, overwhelmed, or overstimulated. A lack of focus for your spiritual energy may leave you feeling unfulfilled or that you lack purpose, where mental energy neglect may lead to boredom. All areas of your life need your attention, and giving one area too much attention while neglecting the rest will also lead to imbalances.

By ensuring balance with your personal energy, you can expect:

Better interpersonal relationships

When you are in control of your thoughts, emotions, and actions, you will be better equipped to handle your relationships with maturity and thoughtfulness. It will assist you in open and honest communication because you are aware and in control of your own energy.

Better physical and mental health

Imbalances in physical, mental, and emotional energy breeds disease and dysfunction. By having balance within your energy, you are looking after your physical energy and health by having and using this energy to keep you healthy (eat right, exercise, etc), you have the mental energy to deal with decisions and solve problems in a calm and logical manner, and you have the emotional energy to deal with conflict and other social situations in a way that will leave you feeling in control and even fulfilled.

Improved work environment

When you are in control of the energy that you put out and your energy is in balance, not only are you able to deal with your colleagues in a positive and collaborative way, but you can work more efficiently. This means a more positive mood when you are at your place of work, and may even result in tangible rewards such as raises or promotions.

FREQUENCIES: NOT JUST FOR YOUR RADIO

When most people think of frequencies, they think of a radio and tuning in to their favorite station. This is actually a great analogy for the frequencies that we will be discussing now, but we will get to that later.

First, let's discuss how energy and frequencies are related. Remember when we said that everything is made of energy, including you? To be more specific, we, and everything around us, are made up of energy-producing particles, which are in a state of constant motion, or in other words, these particles are always vibrating and generate what is known as electromagnetic energy waves. The speed at which these particles vibrate is known as a frequency.

What's really interesting is that the speed and rhythm of these vibrations can differ even in the various cells in your body. Studies have found that this electromagnetic energy and associated vibrations can cause changes in your cells, which in turn has an effect on your body and how it functions (Stanborough, 2020.)

So why does this matter and how does this link into frequencies? Well, the speed of the vibrations of your cells (or frequency) and electromagnetic energy can be influenced by outside factors. In a physical sense, this could be temperature or light, but it goes further than that. You could, in fact, make these vibrations faster or slower, also known as raising or lowering your vibration, by actively altering the way you think, your actions, and even your environment.

So if you are vibrating and producing electromagnetic waves, does that mean everything around us is as well? Yes! And because you are made up differently than your cat, your house, and even the trees outside, they are all vibrating at different frequencies to you. This also means that the vibrational energy of people, places, and the things around you can affect you and your vibrational energy.

Think of walking into a party, not really feeling like it, and wishing that you'd stayed home in your pjs. But then you walk through the door and you feel the energy of the room, the joy, and fun of the people around you, and the company of your friends and suddenly, your mood is uplifted and you are excited to be there. Walking into that environment raised your vibrational energy and you became "in sync" with the energy of your surroundings.

So why would you want to vibrate at a higher or lower frequency? In general, positive emotions, good health, and mental wellbeing are associated with higher vibrations, while negative emotions, disease, and mental illness are associated with lower vibrations.

Within manifestation, this also ties in with the "like attracts like" law. Things, people, and places with a higher vibration will be attracted to you and vice versa if you yourself have a high vibration.

However, it's important to note that this does not mean that if you experience disease, mental illness, or negative emotions that you have a permanently low vibration or that you are not doing enough to raise it. None of these things should bring any shame or guilt.

When your body and mind are not in tune with your true self, this can cause disease and dysfunction. The great news is that raising your frequency has been shown to aid in healing your body, combating disease, and bringing balance back to your body

Attempting to raise your vibration will assist you in attracting the type of life that you wish for and manifesting situations that will make your life better.

RAISING YOUR VIBRATION

How does one even go about raising your vibration? There are a few different techniques that you can use to raise your vibration, but it is important to note that not everything might work for you. For example, if meditation makes you more stressed than it does relaxed, it's not going to give you the desired outcome, so feel free to use the methods that work for you and ignore the ones that don't.

Eating fresh, healthy foods—having a balanced diet

Think of how you feel after you've eaten an entire pizza. You probably feel lazy and not very energetic, right? Now think about a healthy wrap or salad. You will generally feel more energetic and ready to go. By providing nourishment to our body through a balanced diet with lots of fresh fruits and vegetables, we are raising our vibration and giving our health a boost at the same time. This doesn't mean you have to forgo your favorite comfort food forever, just make it more of an exception than a rule.

Getting some exercise and moving your body

When you exercise, you are not only raising your vibration, but getting rid of stagnant energy. Exercise also has the added benefit of being good for your body, your mental state, and is a great way to deal with negative emotions. If you're feeling angry and frustrated, nothing beats a good run or taking out your frustrations on a punching bag. The added bonus being that nobody is going to know that you're imagining your boss's face as the punching bag.

Meditation

Another great technique to raise your vibration is meditation. Not only is it good for slowing down the body and mind, but it is a useful tool for manifestation too. So when you're doing a manifestation meditation, you're actually working to raise your vibration at the same time. Talk about killing two birds with one stone! Meditation has also been linked with helping you to manage and regulate your emotions, so if this is something you struggle with, give it a try. There are plenty of different methods and techniques available for meditation, so if one doesn't work for you, try different options until you find one that suits you.

Go out and experience nature

When we are out in nature, not only does it raise our vibration, but it has a host of positive effects on our physical and mental wellbeing. It lowers your stress hormones and your blood pressure, reduces your fatigue, and helps you find mental clarity. Just think back to the last time you went for a hike or sat on a bench in the park. Just thinking of the peace that it brings ought to give you some idea of how beneficial it is! Additionally, if you are spiritually inclined, it can help you feel more aligned with mother earth and get in touch with the essence of the universe. Something I personally like to do is to take off my shoes and feel the earth beneath my feet. Connecting directly with the earth can be very powerful (it's also known as "earthing" or "grounding".) This technique has been known to help chronic conditions and improve your mood.

Gratitude and Generosity

Practicing gratitude and actively being thankful for the lives that we live is another great technique that raises your vibration and functions as a manifestation tool. It can also lower stress and improve your mental wellbeing. Likewise, being generous through charity, being kind to your community and strangers, or helping animals is another good way to raise your vibration. Like gratitude, as a prosocial behavior, it reduces your stress and may even help you live longer according to a 2013 study (Poulin, Brown, Dillard, & Smith 2013).

Nurturing Healthy Relationships

This ties in with the "like attracts like" and the idea that high frequency people attract high frequency people. If you nurture your relationships with your family, friends, and even colleagues, you will be creating a high vibration environment in which you can all thrive. This doesn't mean that you need to cut people out of your life if your relationship isn't ideal (unless they are extremely toxic and/or abusive, of course.) Everyone goes through their ups and downs after all, so expecting perfection isn't realistic. What it does mean is that you actively work on your relationships and help elevate them to a place where they bring everyone involved joy and put you all on a good frequency together.

Feed Your Passions

This is something a lot of people struggle with, as our society tends to put so much emphasis on everything that you do being 'useful' or 'lucrative.' If you have a passion or hobby like writing, painting, singing, tabletop gaming, cycling, reading, interpretative dance, or absolutely anything else, put some time aside to do it. Doing things that we enjoy raises our vibration and gives us joy, fulfillment, and a feeling of accomplishment. The best part is that you don't even have to be an expert or particularly skilled at these things. As long as you enjoy doing something, it's worth doing, even if you do it 'badly.' You may find that you do improve with repetition or practice, but the important thing to remember is that it doesn't matter either way; your enjoyment is the most important part of the activity.

ENERGY HEALING

As we've established, the frequencies and vibrations of our thoughts and actions have an effect on us and those around us (and vice versa.) This knowledge has allowed for the creation of a specialized healing therapy based on using one's energy to heal another using a variety of techniques.

Energy healing may include modalities such as Reiki, therapeutic touch, and healing touch. These therapies all work in a similar way, with the practitioner assessing their patient's energy fields and then either lightly laying their hands on their body or gently passing them over the various areas to remove energetic blockages and help energy flow.

The specific techniques used in these modalities can be quite varied. Some practitioners use the chakra system, choosing to focus on the various chakra points in their practice, others use pressure point techniques, and some practices even require mental and verbal participation from the patient.

Regardless of the specific techniques used, energy healing can be helpful in healing the body, mind, and spirit of many needing such assistance. If you feel that you are having trouble raising your vibration, an energy healer may be able to assist you in removing any energetic blockages that could be hampering your efforts.

The benefits of energy healing are even starting to be seen as a legitimate complementary therapy that can help patients heal in a more holistic way within medical practices.

5

MANIFESTATION MAGIC—A LITTLE HOCUS POCUS

Now for the part you've all been waiting for! We're going to delve into manifestation magic! It's time to explore what magical correspondences are and why they matter; we're going to give you the tools to design your very own manifestations spell. In addition, we're going to give you important pointers on how to protect yourself from nasties when working magic (yes, nasties do exist and no you don't want to see them), and finally, we're going to discuss why respect is integral in all magical practice.

MAGICAL CORRESPONDENCES

As we've mentioned in an earlier chapter, magical correspondences are essentially things that "go together" and attract certain energies. Remember that rule of "like attracts like?" This is a similar concept except that it extends to every natural thing on Earth and each item will have its own set of correspondences. Putting things that correspond together in rituals assists in directing the energy of your ritual and attracting the right kind of energy to your intention. Even though correspondences are very important to some practitioners, the most important element of magic will always be your will and intent, so don't despair if using correspondences doesn't come naturally at first or if you don't feel comfortable with it and decide not to use it. You already contain all the magic you need.

Some basic correspondences to know are the days of the week:

Day	Planet Correspondence	Magical Work
Monday	Moon	Intuition, Peace, Dream work, Psychic growth, Divination, Spiritual awareness, Conception, Nurturing magic, Emotional magic
Tuesday	Mars	Courage, Conflict, Strength, Protection, Vengeance, Competition, Passion, Vitality
Wednesday	Mercury	Communication, Travel, Wisdom, Divination, Study, Learning
Thursday	Jupiter	Luck, Money, Generosity, Loyalty, Prosperity, Expansion, Fortune
Friday	Venus	Creativity, Love, Fertility, Pleasure, Relationships, Friendships
Saturday	Saturn	Endings, Work, Boundaries, Restrictions, Death, Transformation, Rebirth, Mourning, Wills, Long Life
Sunday	Sun	Healing, Authority, Expansion, Divine Inspiration, Energy, Prosperity, Life Force

The next set of commonly used correspondences are the lunar cycles. This gives you an indication of how to harness lunar energy to power your spells and what phase is good for your specific intention.

New Moon

This is when there seems to be no moon in the sky at all. This can be a good time to do magic to do with beginnings. Are you starting a new job, a new relationship, a new diet regime, or hobby? This is the time to give power to those things. This phase is also a great time to set your goals and intentions for the month, which will 'grow' as the moon gets bigger and fuller throughout the month. With new moons, it can also be good to do what is known as "shadow work." Shadow work is when you examine your traumas, triggers, and behaviors that don't serve you and attempt to understand where they come from, work through them, and subsequently heal in order to grow.

Waxing Moon

This is when the moon is gradually getting larger in the sky and constitutes all the stages between a thin sliver and right before it becomes full. The way to tell if it is in its waxing (growing) or waning (getting smaller) stage is to see what side the light side is on. If it looks like a capital 'D' or the light is on the right side then it is waxing. If it looks like a 'C' or the light is on the left side, then it is waning. The waxing moon is a great time to give energy to your goals that you want to manifest in abundance. Think about the things that you want to "get bigger." You want your career, money, love and relationships, health, and self-esteem etcetera all to grow. So this is the time to help send more energy to these manifestations and goals.

Full Moon

The full moon has intense and powerful energy that can

be used to empower whatever spell or ritual that you decide to do to the absolute max. There's no specific magic that corresponds with the full moon, so you are free to decide what goals or magic you believe requires a large dose of potency. Some witches also decide to charge their crystals or talismans with it or even create moon water by leaving water out in the moonlight and using it in rituals later. As this is also the time that your intuition will be the most "tuned in," it is time to listen to your gut on any decisions or situations that you may be facing. If something doesn't feel right on the night of a full moon, trust your instinct and either remove yourself from the situation or rethink your actions for the evening.

Waning Moon

The waning moon is when the moon is getting smaller again and making its way back around to the new moon phase. As the moon is seemingly 'disappearing,' so too is this a time to use magic to remove things from your life. You could focus on banishing negativity or toxic people from your life or cutting cords (attachments) with things that are bad for you, your personal growth, and your happiness. This could be banishing toxicity at work, losing weight, cutting the cord from a harmful/abusive friendship or relationship, or even banishing self-doubt and poor self-esteem.

The elements are another commonly used part of rituals, and they too have their correspondences that you can use to guide and empower your rituals:

Element	Color	Items To Represent	Uses/ Correspondences
Fire	Red	fire on candles or lanterns, bonfires, images of fire, lighters, matches, volcanic stones, ash, wand, sun images, Strength tarot card	transformation, passion, adolescence, drive, creativity, force, light (illumination), anger, masculinity, energy
Water	Blue/Green	water in a bowl/chalice, seashell, seaweed, mirror, goblet, images of mermaids or bodies of water, Ace of Cups tarot card	healing, cleansing, femininity, emotions, mystery, compassion, slow transformation, secrets, magic, adulthood
Earth	Green/Brown /Gray	rocks, crystals, salt, plants, metal, pentacle, soil, sand, food, cauldron, acorns, seeds, horns/bone, images of trees, Ace of Pentacles tarot card	stability, foundation building, fertility, money, death, growth, grounding, peace, nourishment, gardening, agriculture
Air	Yellow/Gold	incense, feathers, smoke, windchimes, bell, fan, instruments, images of clouds, the sky, angels, fairies, birds or winged insects, Ace of Swords tarot card	inspiration, communication, mobility, writing, youth, enlightenment, computers, electronics, freedom, travel, release

For every herb/essential oil, crystal, and type of incense there are also correspondences, but we will give you the lowdown on all the basic correspondences of those and how to use them in Chapter 6.

The most important thing to remember is that you don't need to learn and recall all these things out of your head. Referencing these correspondences won't make your magic any less powerful. Your will and focus will be the major catalyst and source of power, regardless of how many correspondences you decide to make use of.

HOW TO DESIGN YOUR OWN MANIFESTATION SPELL

Designing your own manifestation spell is not only rewarding, but the very act of creating the ritual yourself will make it more powerful as you are putting your energy toward it from the very beginning.

The very first thing that you'll need to do when you design your own manifestation spell is consider what your goal is. What do you want the spell to achieve, and do you mind how it is achieved?

Sometimes, it's a good idea to take a little time to define the goal. Meditate on it and also consider your reasons behind it. Think about if there are any negative emotions attached to this goal and why they might be present, as they may end up influencing the ritual or the outcome if they are not first addressed. For example, if you are doing a ritual to progress in your career, but you feel guilty or uncomfortable about it because you don't know if you really deserve it, this will certainly come through in the magic that you do and can affect the outcome negatively.

Additionally, are the reasons for your goal in line with your values? Sometimes, we are temporarily blinded by emotion, and if we immediately act on these emotions, we tend to do things that we may not do under normal circumstances (things that may cause us guilt or regret.)

Once you have your goal firmly in your mind, the next step is deciding what kind of magic you want to do and how much time you have to do it. If you only have 15 minutes free then you might want to choose something like a spell jar, candle magic, a magically charged bath, or quick rituals that include few components. If you have more time, you can design an entire ritual that includes incantations or invocations, setting up a circle, raising energy, and more.

It is important to note that just because your magical workings may be short in duration, it doesn't make it less powerful. As long as you bend your will and intent towards your goal while doing it and don't let yourself become distracted, it should be just as effective.

To create a spell jar, you'll need a glass, plastic, or metal jar or bottle (glass is quite popular because you can see everything inside, but it's your choice), some sage incense or salt, and then your spell components, which we will come to in a moment. The first step is to cleanse your jar or bottle by letting the sage incense smoke fill the bottle or by filling it with salt overnight (the former is a more popular method as the latter can be messy.)

Let the smoke dissipate or pour the salt out (please do not pour any salt on soil, plants, or nature of any kind; it will cause harm to them), and then focus for a moment or two on your goal, holding it in your mind. Then one by one, place your spell components into the jar, thinking of their correspondences and why you chose them as you do so.

Your spell components may include certain herbs, crystals, natural items such as feathers, or rocks, that may represent the elements, paper with runes, sigils, or your specific goal written on it. We will come to the correspondences of specific herbs and crystals in the next chapter, but for example, if you are doing a spell to strengthen your relationship and you chose rose quartz for romance, lavender for peace and closeness, ash to represent fire's passion, and either a picture of you and your partner together or your goal written on a piece of paper, you will focus on what you want each component to bring to the spell as you place them inside.

Once everything has been added, you can take a moment to visualize what you want your goal to look like and how it will come to be, or even choose to say it out loud and describe it. If you would prefer to say a prayer to your deity to lend their strength to the spell, that is also perfect.

Once this is done, you will close the jar or bottle with a cork or lid and use melted candle wax to seal the spell jar. Usually, the color of candle will correspond with your spell's intention, (so if it's for your relationship, you may choose red or pink.) Keep this jar in a place that you will be able to see it if possible, or otherwise in a safe place where it won't be broken.

For another quick method of manifesting, you can simply write your goal on a piece of paper or a bay leaf, burn incense that corresponds with your goal, and focus on your goal and how it will be achieved (or say it out loud/pray) while you either burn it (safely) or bury it in the garden. Usually, fire will manifest things a little quicker but may not be as long lasting, while burying things in soil will manifest more slowly, but will likely be a longer lasting result. Consider your goal when deciding which to choose.

Perhaps one of the quickest methods is by using candle magic. You can choose to anoint a candle with essential oils, herbs, or crystals that correspond with your goals or simply choose a candle color that corresponds with your goal. Then simply visualize the goal and how it will be achieved, or say it out loud/pray, and light the candle. Whenever the candle is alight, it should be considered to be working your will. Please be careful with lit candles; do not leave them unattended and be sure that they are not near anything flammable or in reach of pets and children. We only want spiritual raging fires, not literal ones.

Designing a full ritual is a little more work but can be very rewarding and give you confidence in your manifestation

MANIFESTING MAGIC

magic. You don't have to work in a circle, but it is usually recommended for newbie practitioners as it helps keep you safe from outside energetic influences, and keeps errant magic from going places you don't want it to go.

The first step to creating a ritual is finding a safe place where you won't be disturbed. Being outside in nature can be a lovely environment for a ritual, so if you have a garden or secluded park, please feel free to use these spaces as long as you are safe and won't have people close enough to distract you.

The next step is to 'cleanse' yourself or prepare your mind for the ritual. You can do this through meditation, through visualization, (imagine all the negative emotions and baggage of the day leaving your mind), or through an actual bath or shower. If you opt for the actual bath or shower, letting any negative or distracting thoughts go and imagining yourself being cleansed of any energetic baggage as you wash yourself will help you to get into the correct mindset. Try to hold your ritual and the goal of it in your mind once you've rid yourself of unwanted thoughts and energy.

Once you've decided on the area you'd like to do your ritual, you will need to cleanse it. Before you bust out a rake or a mop, this is a spiritual cleansing so you can either smudge the area with sage (go around the area with sage incense or a smudge stick), or you can use your besom (broom) to sweep out any negative energy. When using the besom, you won't actually be sweeping the ground but will be sweeping just above it. Having said this, it is best to be working in a physically clean area as well, so if you're on a carpet and it needs a vacuum, then by all means, do so.

Then you need to set up your ritual space with your spell components and implements. Many rituals include a representation of the elements, which are chosen according to the goal of your ritual. So for example, the representation of the earth element can be a crystal that corresponds with the goal of your ritual; the representation of the fire element can be a colored candle that will correspond with your goal of the the ritual; the air element can be represented by incense that corresponds with the goal of your ritual and so on.

The way that your elements are set up can be via the four cardinal directions that are associated with the elements (more on that below), or in the shape of a pentagram, which also represents the elements with the additional element of 'spirit,' which can be used to represent your deity if you have one and want to invoke them during the ritual.

- Fire - South
- Earth - North
- Air - East
- Water - West

A pentagram is a five-pointed star with a circle around it. The elements represented on a pentagram, listing them in a clockwise direction from the lowest point on the left are: Earth, Air, Spirit, Water, Fire.

Use whichever configuration works for you and makes the most sense, as this is a personal choice. You may also choose not to represent the four elements at all.

If you will be using any tools or ingredients, like your athame, rope/string, photographs, wand, candles etc, place them within reach, close to where the center of the circle will be so that you can easily reach them where you sit or stand within the circle.

If you have written something for the ritual and you have trouble memorizing it, bring it in with you. As long as you feel the words and speak them with meaning, there's no reason you can't use your notes as an aid. Not everyone has a great memory for these sorts of things after all!

Once everything is in place, you can start drawing your circle. Some practitioners choose to start their circle in the East because it is from whence the sun rises, while others choose the North because it is associated with the Earth, where the circle begins, but you can start your circle at any point that makes you comfortable or makes sense to you.

Many choose to begin with a physical circle, which is then used as a focal point to start putting the energetic circle in place. You can use ground eggshells, stones, plants, flowers, chalk, or a circle of salt (but again, please do not use salt in any natural environment as it will be harmful to the soil and plants there.) Make the circle as big or small as you feel will make you comfortable, but remember to leave yourself enough space for all the activities that you will be doing within it (if you are going to be dancing, make the circle a little bigger.)

Always make your circle from the inside (that is, with you in it.) When you produce a circle in this way, it means that you are creating a space of sacred power and protection for yourself, so it is generally considered a bad idea to break or step over the circle before you have completed your ritual.

You can either use visualization as you are creating the physical embodiment of the circle or do so afterwards with your finger, your wand, or your athame (this will be done by pointing at the circle; you needn't physically touch it.) When creating the energetic portion of your circle, you can envision your circle as a forcefield, as vines, as fire, as water, as a shimmering white sphere, whatever you feel will protect you, and you will visualize it forming from the physically drawn circle and then building to create a dome that completely encloses you from above and below.

Once your circle has been created, you start the actual spell that you created this ritual space for. The specifics of the spell are usually representative in nature, which means that you will do actions to represent your goal. If you wish to cut ties or your attachment with a person, place, or thing, you may bring a physical cord and your boline to cut it, a physical representation of the removal of the attachment. If you want to manifest something or want it to 'grow,' you may plant a seed, or fill up a cup, or other physical representations of growing and increasing. Sometimes you may want to use a focal point that ties to a person, place, or relationship, so you may use a photograph, a piece of jewelry, some hair, or a business card. The most important part of putting your spell together is that *you* understand and believe in the symbolism of what each action represents. It doesn't have to come from ancient books or texts to be an effective spell; it just needs to gel well with your intent and make sense in your mind.

Once your spell is complete, you have the option to raise energy. Some practitioners feel that they expend enough energy during the actual spell itself while others like to have a part of the ritual where they focus solely on raising their personal energy towards powering the spell because they find it difficult to raise this energy while performing the spell. This, again, will completely depend on what you prefer.

To raise energy, you keep your goal firmly in your mind while you dance, drum, sing, meditate, chant, or do any other action that is used to generate energy. You might feel it building up inside your body like excitement or anticipation that you can't contain. Hold that energy inside yourself for as long as possible, and then when you can't any longer, release it while holding your goal firmly in mind to send that energy to power your spell. Some release it by pointing their finger at their spell (if for example, you cut a rope, then at the rope, or at the glass that you used); others hold their arms open and just let the energy flow toward their goal that they are concentrating on. Do whatever feels right to release the energy.

The next step is very important; that is grounding the energy. After raising the energy, you may still have a lot of it swirling around inside you like a turbulent pool. You want to ground yourself and excess energy, both to prevent accidentally sending energy in an unintended direction or person, and to help get your personal energy back to normal. Many people can feel jumpy, jittery, or even a little anxious after a ritual because of the excess energy. Others may feel drained or exhausted, so this grounding technique is a way to normalize your personal energy before going about the rest of your day.

To ground the energy and yourself, you can sit down or (if the circle space allows) lie down and meditate or visualize all the energy draining from you into the floor below you. This works very well if you are outside, as connecting directly to the earth is a great way to ground yourself. If you are outside, the feel of the grass or earth beneath your feet can be a very grounding experience.

You can also direct your energy into any of your tools for future use, be that your athame, your wand, or a candle. Hold the tool in your hands and visualize the energy leaving you and entering into the object. Another common way to ground oneself is to eat and drink something. If your practice is not religious, this can be a cracker and water, bread and wine, juice and cookies, anything small and easy to consume. For certain religions, there are certain foods and drinks that are traditional, but you can find this out from those in your church or community.

Once you feel grounded and calm, you can begin the last step, which is breaking down the circle. This is a similar process to creating the circle and will usually involve both visualizing your protective dome (however you imagine it), to recede into the physical circle on the ground. Then you can sweep away, clean off, or otherwise remove the physical aspects that marked the boundary of your circle. Once this has been completed, you can take all your tools and components back inside to be stored. If you have ashes, or components that you would like to dispose of, if they are not harmful to the earth (ashes, water, etcetera), you can dispose of them outside or bury them. If they are not, you can simply throw them away in the bin. If you are unsure if something is safe to put in the ground or throw away, feel free to look it up (if you pour liquid wax down your sink, you're going to have a bad time.)

After all your things have been packed away, you can sweep the area once again with your besom (broom) to fully cleanse the space. If you are outside, this may not be necessary as the energy will be absorbed into the natural environment.

HOW TO PROTECT YOURSELF WHEN WORKING WITH MAGIC

When performing any kind of magic, whether it is a full-blown ritual or a quick and simple spell, it is important to protect yourself from unwanted energies, negative side-effects from your spell, or harmful entities.

Shielding is a technique that allows you to protect yourself from unwanted energies and can actually be done at any time (not just when working magic.) Similar but easier than the circle in a ritual, it simply requires that you visualize a barrier around yourself, either as a bubble (yes, like Bubble Boy), or as a second skin that fits your form. This shield can look any way that will make you feel most protected. Whether it's a forcefield like in Star Wars, a fiery wall, a mirror, or even something like a whirlwind. When doing any kind of magic, take a moment to put your shielding in place, and then once you are done, you can let it drop away. You can also do this when you feel like other people's negative energy around you is affecting you, whether at work or at home.

Grounding is another technique that was covered within ritual creation but is equally as important to help you release negative and unwanted energies. As with shielding, while good to do before and after performing any magic, it can be very helpful to do during daily life as well. If for example you've had a fight with someone and you feel that this bad energy is lingering, grounding is a great way to get rid of it.

To ground bad energy, you can either go outside and stand with your bare feet or your head on the grass or soil and imagine the negative energy flowing out into the ground. You can also have a shower and imagine the water taking the energy away with it and going down the drain. Breathing the bad energy out during a breathing exercise or meditation or literally just shaking it off by either shaking your hands or even your whole body (to the song "Shake It Off" if you want) is another great way to ground yourself and rid yourself of the bad juju.

Grounding before a spell can help get rid of energy that you don't want affecting your spell or outcome, and doing it afterward can just help to normalize your energy if you're feeling drained or jumpy.

RESPECT—FIND OUT WHAT IT MEANS TO ME

Now that you have all the tools to create your own rituals and spells to manifest the dreams of your life, there is one last thing to keep in mind before you go forth and conquer.

Magic is exciting and very personal, and it's not necessarily religious, which also means that it might not always be as somber or serious as common religious practices. Additionally, the religions that do practice magic are also often a little more free, go with the flow types (not always.)

There's nothing wrong with this, and in fact, levity and laughter are great practices within magic and manifestation. It's good for the soul to have fun and let yourself free to be joyful.

This being said, magic is not a toy, or a joke. It mustn't be done lightly or flippantly. Your personal energy and the energy of those around you should be respected. Any area that you do magic in, particularly if it's a natural environment, should be respected. Calling on spirits or the deities must also only be done if you are serious about making contact with them and in a respectful manner. Doing otherwise will only provoke misfortune.

As everyone knows by now, "with great power comes great responsibility" (even when you're not Spiderman.)

6

HOW TO USE HERBS, ESSENTIAL OILS, AND CRYSTALS TO SUPPORT MANIFESTATION

Now that you're armed with the knowledge of how to make your very own rituals, you can enter the exciting world of herbs, crystals, essential oils, and more! In this chapter, you will be given the correspondences of the basics of these items as well as how you can use them in your magical manifestations. Additionally, you will learn about sigils and how you can make your very own from scratch to support your spells and manifestation magic.

FANTASTIC HERBS AND HOW TO USE THEM

As there are entire books written on the correspondences and uses of herbs within magical practice, below is just a collection of the most basic and commonly used that are generally considered safe to work with. If you plan on ingesting any herbs, please be aware of any cautionary notes on whether they are actually edible or not, and be sure to look out for any symptoms of allergic reaction if you've never ingested or handled the herb before. If you suspect you are having an allergic reaction to herbs that you have touched or ingested, please contact a doctor immediately.

Herb	Correspondences	Uses	Edible
Angelica	cleansing, consecrating, protection, blessing, healing, luck	scents, amulets, food, potions, baths, sachets, oils, incense, washes	Yes
Apple	love	food, amulets, potions	Yes
Barley	fertility, faery offering	food, potion, amulet	Yes
Bay Leaf	protection, divination	food seasoning, baths, amulets, sachets, washes, oils, scents, living plant	No (Set aside before eating food seasoned with bay leaf)
Chamomile	healing, protection, blessing, magical dreamwork, reducing stress or sadness	washes, oils, amulets, sachets, baths, living plants, scents	Yes
Cinnamon	clearing limits, protection, expanding horizons	food seasoning, amulets, incense, washes, oils, scents, sachets	Yes
Coriander	protection, independance	food seasoning, amulets, baths, incense, washes, potions, sachets, oils, scents	Yes

Herb	Correspondences	Uses	Edible
Dill	prosperity, protection, clearing the mind, raising the spirits, banishing, blessing	oils, washes, baths, food seasoning, amulets, sachets, scents	Yes
Fennel	success, magical healing, blessing, protection	food seasoning, potions, amulets, sachets, washes, baths, scents, oils	Yes
Garlic	banishes evil, protection, health, happiness, success	food seasoning, amulets	Yes
Ginger	healing, stimulates sexual energy, protection	food seasoning, potions, amulets, sachets, baths, washes, incense, oil, scents	Yes
Jasmine	sexual magics, love, protection, healing, banishes sadness	oils, amulets, baths, scents, sachets, incense, washes	No
Lavender	soothes, restores balance, psychic work, visionary work, dream work, calming	oils, scents, sachets, incense, washes, baths, amulets, living plants	No
Mugwort	prophetic dreams, psychic powers, protection	baths, washes, amulets, sachets, oils, scents, incense, potions	Yes

Herb	Correspondences	Uses	Edible
Rose	love, speed up magic, compassion, devotion, relationships	food, baths, amulets, oils, scents, washes, sachets, incense, potions	Yes
Rosemary	love, remembrance, good sleep, protection, banish nightmares, banish spirits	food seasoning, living plant, sachets, washes, amulets, potions, incense, baths, scents, oils	Yes
Sage	purification, consecration, wisdom, cleansing	foods, scents, seasoning, amulets, living plants, baths, washes, incense, sachets, oil	Yes
Sweet Basil	compassion, ends bickering and feuds, courage, banish hostile spirits, purification, protection, banish fear, weakness, or confusion	living plants, amulets, sachets, incense, seasoning for food, potions, baths, washes, oils, scents	Yes
Thyme	psychic abilities, prophetic dreams, protection, purifying, faery magic	food seasoning, oils, scents, washes, incense, living plants, amulets, baths, sachets, potions	Yes
Valerian	repels negativity, protection, purification, cleansing, blessing	scents, amulets, baths, potions, washes, sachets, oils, incense	Yes (in moderation)

Herb	Correspondences	Uses	Edible
Vervain	visionary work, inspiration, protection, increases effect of magic, success	oils, living plants, amulets, incense, sachets, potions, baths, washes	Yes
Yarrow	happy marriage, love	oils, amulets, sachets, baths, washes, scents	No

CRAZY FOR CRYSTALS

As with herbs, there are thousands of different crystals out there (and entire books written on their magical correspondences and uses), so we have included the basics for you to get started with in your magical practice. As you expand, or if you find you have a greater interest in crystals, you can research or buy books that focus on a greater variety of crystals. I will be publishing a detailed book on crystals and their magical uses in the future (if you would be so kind as to rate this book, it will help me to keep the books flowing!).

As with any magic, crystal magic is not always for everyone. Every person has a vocation of magic which they fall in love with instantly and others that they just don't connect with, so if any of these don't work for you, know that you'll find something that will.

Crystals can be used in spell bottles/bags, spells, rituals, in your bath/shower (if they are not damaged by water), next to your bed, under your pillow, in strategic areas in your home, or in a tea bag/receptacle in your teapot or water bottle (so that it lends energy to your drink; please don't swallow or eat your crystals!). Crystals can also adorn your magical tools or act like talismans in jewelry. You can also just pop them into your pockets (or, if you're a lady, your bra); you don't necessarily have to wear them to reap the benefits of their energy. For beautification or health effects, you can use them in a face roller, a gua sha stone, or during massage.

Crystals	Correspondences
Agate	healing, wealth, protection, insight
Amber	protection, healing, luck, magic amplifier
Amethyst	happiness, dreaming, psychic enhancer, mental clarity
Aventurine	perception, luck, money
Bloodstone	strength, courage, victory, healing
Carnelian	vitality, health, protection, confidence, mental clarity, ambition, energy
Chalcedony	banishes nightmares, peace, mental balance
Chrysoprase	success, luck, happiness, friendship
Citrine	dreaming, protection, psychic enhancer, abundance, joy, positivity
Coral	power, healing, protection
Diamond	peace, loyalty, harmony, energy source, banishing
Emerald	mental power, money, love, banish illusions, divination clarity
Garnet	strength, healing, protection
Hematite	divination, grounding, concentration
Jade	longevity, wisdom, healing, weather magic, good luck, abundance
Jasper	tenacity, protection, dispels hostile magic and spirits
Jet	divination, shielding, protection
Lapis Lazuli	love, healing, protection
Moonstone	dream control, astral control, divination, psychic enhancer
Obsidian	focus, clarity, contemplation, logic, protection
Onyx	balancing sex drive, protection, counter-magic
Opal	power, astral protection, luck, scrying

Crystals	Correspondences
Pearl	wealth, good fortune, love
Quartz	mental clarity, focus, emotional stability, psychic enhancer, master healing stone
Rose quartz	love, compassion, relationships
Ruby	power, wealth, vitality, protection, clarity, focus
Tiger's Eye	courage, protection, energy, abundance, safe travels
Topaz	wealth, healing, love, protection, happiness
Tourmaline	business, relationships, friendships, love
Turquoise	money, courage, friendship, love, protection

ESSENTIAL OILS, NOT JUST FOR YOUR BATH

Essential oils are oils that are extracted from plants. These oils are both fragrant, retaining the scent of the plant that they were extracted from, in addition to retaining some of the benefits that the plant would have on the human body.

Essential oils can be used in a variety of ways, but they are NOT to be ingested. When used on the skin, they must be within a cream or carrier oil; they should never be applied directly to the skin without being added to an oil-based medium first.

These oils can be used in a similar way to incense, and some practitioners even prefer to burn them instead of incense, as the smell can be slightly more subtle and it will be easier to mix and match the oils you want for a particular purpose.

Essential oils can be used in the bath or shower, in creams and tinctures, on your pillowcase or bedding, in spell jars, in rituals, in your shampoo or conditioner, and of course in diffusers or humidifiers (remember to check if your humidifier can handle essential oils first as it may damage the parts in some models.)

Essential oils can sometimes be used as substitutions for the plants or herbs you would have used in magic and vice versa, and as such, you will see that the correspondences of the plants and essential oils will be virtually the same. However, the commonly used herbs and commonly used essential oils do not always overlap, so we will be sharing the information on the oils you don't already have from the herbs section.

Essential Oil	Correspondences
Bergamot	success, energy
Cloves	courage, power, protection
Eucalyptus	purification, healing
Frankincense	stress, meditation, spirituality
Honeysuckle	intuition, psychic enhancer, prosperity
Lavender	relaxation, aids insomnia and anxiety
Neroli	energy, happiness, joy
Oakmoss	prosperity, gratitude, abundance
Patchouli	prosperity, sexual energies
Sandalwood	all-purpose
Ylang-ylang	love, sexual desires, happiness

HOW TO MAKE AND USE SIGILS

For starters what is a sigil (pronounced si-jil by the way)? It is a magical symbol that is basically shorthand for an outcome, goal, or your will. For example, you can create a sigil for protection, for love, for money, and other generalized goals, or you can even create a sigil for getting a raise, for losing weight in a healthy way, or for being more sexually desirable to your partner. So you can be as specific or general in your intent as you want. You can use sigils made by other people if you absolutely aren't interested in creating them yourself but still want to use them, but, as with most things in magic, it is much more effective (and fun) if you create any sigils you want to use yourself.

So how are sigils used? They can be painted onto doors, any surface in your house, on or in your books, on yourself in cream, as symbols used in your spells or rituals, on rocks outside yours or someone else's house, and if you're really invested in a sigil, even as a tattoo. As you can see, you can use a sigil pretty much anywhere, with anything (obviously take into account what you're putting it on; don't use anything toxic on your skin or damaging on your furniture), on anything. Please don't put sigils on people or their belongings without their consent; always ask first.

Now the exciting part, how are sigils made? There are actually a few different ways to go about it, and all of them are correct. The first step in all of them is coming up with the phrase or goal that you want to manifest and make it as short and concise as possible. So if you want a raise, you say, "I'll get a raise," not "I will advance my career such that my employer desires to give me a raise" (good on you if you have mastered the corporate language, though.) The next step is where the techniques vary.

One way to make your sigil is to use these letters in an artful arrangement, with some being backwards and upside down and others being on top of each other to create a symbol. This method really takes practice to make it look nice, so don't despair if it's not a work of art immediately. If you want examples of such sigils, you can look for 'sigils' on Pinterest and you will get an idea of how they can look.

Another way is to take your phrase, remove all the vowels, and then remove any repeating consonants. So "I'll get a raise" becomes "lgtrs." Then you plot out a circle, like a clock face, and you put your letters at random places on the clock face. For example, you could put the 'l' in the 2 o'clock position and the 's' at the 7 o'clock position, the 't' at the 11 o'clock position and so on. Then once all your letters are plotted on the 'clock,' you start at a letter and you draw straight lines from one letter to another, in any order, until you have been to every letter once. This should give you something resembling a symbol and you can use circles, lines, and interesting accents to make it attractive to you. Again, it doesn't need to look any specific way; if you like it and it speaks to you (not literally obviously), you've done it correctly.

When you want to use a sigil, you place it on the area or object of your choice and while doing so, hold your outcome in your mind and put your will, intent, and personal power toward it.

To use sigil magic on its own to manifest your outcome, you can put it on a piece of paper, power it with your energy, and burn it. You can do the same but bury the paper in the earth or put it on a rock and toss it into a river or the ocean. You can even charge it and then tear it up or throw it away. The important part of this is to remember to charge it with your energy (intent and will) and to apply your focus.

Once you've performed your sigil magic, it should work on its own so you can just leave it in the universe's hands, no continued focus required!

7

DIVINATION, SCRYING, AND TAROT, OH MY!

The word "divination" may conjure up images of an old gypsy woman gazing at your palm and giving you the lowdown on your future, but in reality, it is much more practical and accessible than that (no old gypsy ladies necessary.) In this chapter, we'll explain what divination is and how it will help you on your road to manifesting your dream life. We'll also give you the basics on methods such as tarot cards and scrying.

WHAT IS DIVINATION? CAN I TELL MY FUTURE?

The first thing that we need to get straight with divination is that you can't use it to tell your future (disappointing I know.) You can get hints of what's ahead and some guidance on the best path forward, but it is by no means a way to accurately plot out what's ahead like some cosmic cheat sheet.

Divination taps into your personal energy and subconscious mind, and some believe that it can also tap into the energy of your spiritual guides, your ancestors, and/or your deities. This means that divination, like most magic, is a personal and unique practice and might be slightly different for everyone.

For some, it might aid them in sorting through their own personal energy, subconscious beliefs, and hidden knowledge to find out what is blocking them in their manifestation of their goals or help clarify a situation that they may feel confused or disturbed by.

Others may perform divination to get guidance from their ancestors, spiritual guides, and/or deities on how to grow spiritually, how to manifest their desires, what obstacles might be blocking them, clarity on confusing situations, and sometimes to grow closer with those entities to improve their collaborative magic and their relationship with them.

Divination can be done in a large number of ways. Some ways are more common to particular magical, geographical, or cultural paths and practices. Divination through bone throwing or using animal entrails are examples of forms of divination that are more specific to particular cultures and specialized magical practices.

More commonly, magical practitioners use methods such as tarot cards, runes, scrying, numerology, and astrology. Every method can be perfected and honed, so how deeply you venture into the practice is up to you. For some people, divination is a tool that they use to gain understanding and guidance only for themselves and their own situations, while others find that it becomes a vocation and they feel they are able and willing to do readings to provide such illumination for others.

An important fact to remember about divination is that it has nothing to do with the cards, the runes, or the crystal ball you use. There is nothing innately special or magical about these objects except that they provide a framework for you to be able to focus your energy and unconscious mind onto. While you can certainly send your energy into your tools and become more attuned to a particular deck of tarot cards or scrying mirror, *you* are the magical part of this equation. Theoretically, with enough practice, you could use a pack of playing cards or the surface of a puddle to perform your divination, because the insight all comes from you (and your ancestors, guides, or deities if this is your path.)

Below we will give you the basics of some of the most common methods of divination (tarot and scrying) and you can see which method works for you and investigate whether you want to take your practice further, or merely use divination when the need arises to give you guidance in times of need.

The clarity that you gain through divination can be an invaluable tool in manifesting your dream life, as it can provide much needed guidance and direction to enhance your manifestation when it's going well, or help you get back on track if you find that your methods are not working or results are too slow for your liking.

TAROT CARDS

Tarot reading is a form of cartomancy (card divination), whereby the practitioner uses a pack of tarot cards to divine insight into the past, present situations, or the future by asking a question and then drawing cards in a certain spread to gain insight from them.

The history and origins of tarot is as mysterious as the history of magic itself. It has been theorized to have originally been either a game, a way to exercise the mind, or a fortune-telling aid. The country of origin has been credited to Spain, the Middle East, Egypt, the Far East, Italy, and Southern France and some others. Neither the actual place of origin nor the original purpose was ever definitively confirmed.

The tarot is made up of 78 cards. The deck is composed of 22 Major Arcana (or Trump) cards and 56 Minor Arcana cards. The Major Arcana have unique and distinguishable names such as The Fool, The Magician, The Empress etcetera, while the Minor Arcana are divided up into four suits (much like playing cards), Wands, Cups, Swords, and Pentacles. In contrast to typical playing cards, the Minor Arcana has four "court" cards, King, Queen, Knight, and Page, as well as the numbers one (ace) to ten.

With tarot becoming more popular in recent years with the expansion of spiritualism, more tarot decks have been created with different "themes" such as Egyptian, Celtic, gods and goddesses, angel cards, or daemon tarot decks. This means that while the general layout is often the same in addition to the cards having an approximate agreement in meaning, there will be some variation depending on the specific deck. For example, the angel cards may have an Angel Gabriel as their Page of Wands card, while another deck might have the Greek god Hermes. They both have the concept of "a special delivery of a message" and "an urge to understand a higher meaning in one's life" in common, but because each deck is using very specific individuals to represent the card, the message might be slightly different than the standard unthemed Page of Wands card.

This means that it's important when acquiring a themed tarot deck that it's a theme that you enjoy and speaks to you on some level, both so you can gain an understanding more quickly as well as genuinely enjoy learning and getting familiar with your deck.

As interpreting tarot is an individual practice, familiarizing yourself with the pictures will also help you get an intuitive feel for the card, as a large part of reading tarot is taking advantage of your intuition and accessing subconscious knowledge and insight.

As tarot reading is such an intuitive and personal art, our guide below will give you the basics of interpreting tarot cards and basic spreads. If you feel that you'd like to further explore this or would prefer a more rigid approach, there are many more in-depth guides specifically on tarot interpretation that have a much more in-depth and/or strict approach to tarot and individual card meanings.

Generally, when a card is reversed (upside down) in a reading, it means the opposite of the usual meanings of the card (if a card represents growth, it might represent a lack of growth), however not all practitioners integrate this into their readings and prefer to read all their cards right-side up, while others prefer to look at all the cards together to get a clear message rather than examine them too closely on an individual basis. You can try both techniques and see what works for you.

The Major Arcana and their meanings are listed below:

Cards	Possible Meanings
The Fool	unexpected influences/situations, sudden opportunities, adventures, escape, the need to let go of old methods/ways and try something new, "Anything could happen"
The Magician	beginnings, action, creative initiative, skill, abundance, you have what you need but haven't started your journey toward your goal yet, new opportunities of creative/intellectual activities, possibilities for new projects, you have all you need to succeed, it is up to you to decide how to use the power and energy you have at your disposal
The Empress	fertility, growth, joyful stable relationships, motherhood, love, marriage, creative pursuits, joy in nurturing (people, projects, art etc)
The Emperor	stability, financial and material success, ambition, authority, achievements, indicates the practical changes and energy required to manifest a goal, indicates a time to take control of your endeavors
The High Priestess	intuition, insight, secrets, unfulfilled potential, something hidden that is yet to come to light, the need to focus on your intuition and gut feelings
The Hierophant	guidance required in spiritual matters, need to find meaning in life, need to understand our calling or higher nature, requirement to study, need for mentorship or classes
The Lovers	love, relationships, choice or trial, choices resulting in a heartfelt solution, crossroads, commitment, partnerships
The Chariot	struggle, journey, confidence, drive, willpower, fight or conflict to reach goal, overcoming obstacles
Justice	balance, weighing up options, find fair solutions, think rationally, to put emotions aside for a decision, fairness, responsibility, cause and effect
Temperance	partnerships, cooperation, friendships, compromise, need for a balanced approach, harmony, moderation, balance
Strength	determination, courage, strength, potential to achieve greatness, discipline, self-control, self-awareness, conviction, potency, virility, vitality
The Hermit	patience, solitude, soul searching, meditation, withdrawal, introspection, self-reflection

Cards	Possible Meanings
The Wheel Of Fortune	luck, big decision, new beginnings, destiny, changes, winning, opportunities
The Hanged Man	sacrifice, understanding, metamorphosis, letting go, suspension, breaking old patterns
Death	endings heralding new beginnings, mortality, extreme change, illness, letting go of attachments
The Devil	repression, obstacles hampering progress, misspent or misdirected energy, temptation, enslavement, feeling trapped, bondage, materialism
The Tower	breaking down to build up, renovation, unexpected change, need to remove rigid structures or false values, accident, destruction
The Star	inspiration, joy, promise, good fortune, hope, optimism, renewal, imagination, good health, opportunities
The Moon	fluctuation, change, uncertainty, illusion, solutions through intuition rather than reason, hidden things, deception, confusion
The Sun	energy, success, happiness, prosperity, true friends, optimism, enlightenment, vitality
Judgment	settlement of a matter, decision making, renewal, clean slate, rewards reaped, awakening, redemption, renewal, transition
The World	harmony, success, achievement, realizing your goals, fulfillment, possibilities, positive conclusions

The Minor Arcana suits and their overall meanings are listed below:

Suite	Meaning or Domain
Wands	intuition, imagination, creativity, spirituality, inspiration, primal energy, passion
Cups	feelings, emotions, relationships, inner life, communication
Swords	intellect, thoughts, logic, truth, decisions, learning
Pentacles	sensation, physical being, material life, reality, finances, physical needs, actions

How to interpret the numbers and court cards of the Minor Arcana are listed below:

Card	Meaning
Aces (Ones)	beginnings, potential, creative power, opportunity
Twos	duality, opposites, balance/conflict, partnership
Threes	growth, expansion, groups, creativity
Fours	logic, reality, reason, structure, manifestation, stability
Fives	uncertainty, volatility, change, instability, conflict
Sixes	harmony, equilibrium, balance, cooperation, communication
Sevens	wisdom, completion, assessment, knowledge, reflection
Eights	regeneration, balance, renewal, mastery, action, accomplishment
Nines	fulfillment, attainment, fruition
Tens	completion, renewal, completion, perfection, end of a cycle

The court cards are a little more complicated than the numbered cards, as they can be read a number of ways. They can be interpreted as a type of person that will play a part in the person's life (yourself or whoever you are doing a reading for), an aspect of the person's personality, or an actual event. This is where you would take into account the position of the card in the spread, the other cards, the impression of the overall message, and of course, your intuition. This comes with practice, so if you stumble on the court cards initially, don't worry. Like any other muscle, your intuition is something that you hone and strengthen over time.

Below there are some indications of how you can interpret the court cards:

Card	Interpretation
Page	a messenger/message, the beginning of an event, a young person, an aspect of personality beginning to develop, immaturity
Knight	movement, action, action-oriented person, seeker personality, youthful go-getter
Queen	mature, motherly, nurturing, compassionate, caring, feminine
King	Authority, dynamic, active, masculine, mature, experienced person

Now that you have the basics of how to interpret the tarot cards, we will explain how you draw the cards, as well as the 'spreads' or configurations that include the number and placement of cards that you can use to gain insight and answer questions.

To draw cards, one usually shuffles the deck well, and then lays them out, picture side down (so you can't see what the cards are), in a fan shape (think magicians when they ask you to pick a card) so that you have access to all the cards. Hover your hand over the cards and let your intuition guide you. You might feel a kind of 'tingle' or 'tugging' sensation, or one card might just look very attractive to you. Pick these cards to the number of the spread you are doing and lay them out accordingly.

Some common spreads include:

One Card Spread

This is the quickest and easiest method and can help you when you don't have time or energy to do a full and involved spread. It involves asking a specific question starting with statements like "what is stopping me from…", "how do I…", "why do I…" etc. Then you pick a card and that card will give you the immediate guidance that you need.

Three Card Spread

This involves picking three cards that can represent:

- Past, present, and future
- Situation, obstacle, and advice
- Mind, body, and spirit

When using the "past, present, future" spread, you can do this to understand a relationship, a situation, a projection of your career, or anything else when you feel that you need to understand a pattern to be able to see the big picture and help you progress.

The "situation, obstacle, advice" spread is relatively self-explanatory, as it can help you better understand a situation, what is blocking you from manifesting your desire, and provide advice on how to move forward with the situation in a positive way.

The "mind, body, spirit" spread can be used when one is looking for a source of imbalance or to find out what each element requires to improve or thrive.

Five Card Spread

Placed in a pattern like the dots on dice (for five), there

are a number of ways to do a five card spread, but a good beginner spread is the following:

1. Present situation
2. Influences
3. Challenges
4. Final Outcome
5. Theme

This will allow you to get an in depth understanding of a situation, relationship, or the state of a particular manifestation.

Regardless of the spread or deck that you use, tarot can prove very useful in guiding you in your manifestations on your journey to your best life.

SCRYING - LOOK INTO MY CRYSTAL BALL

This form of divination commonly involves the use of an opaque or reflective surface, but some have used tools like fire, so it depends on your preference.

This is a much more free-form version of divination that requires you to clear your mind, rather than focus too much on asking specific questions or looking for anything in particular.

Many practitioners like to start with meditation, drumming, chanting, or breathing exercises to get them into a trance state. Once you're in the trance state, you can look into a bowl of water, a fire, a mirror, a crystal/glass ball, a lake/river, or anything opaque or reflective.

Let your gaze soften, don't concentrate too hard, and watch the surface for as long as you can. Most beginners don't start to see anything before 10-15 minutes so just be patient and don't try to force it.

When images do come, let them flow; don't try to make sense of them immediately, but try your best to remember them. Once you've finished the scrying exercise, write down everything that you saw.

Sometimes, the things you see will be symbols representing something else. Once you've come out of your trance state, you can sit and review what you've written down and think about what the images could mean or how they relate to you. For some, the images are very direct and clearcut, while for others, it can be a bit more vague and a little confusing.

Practice helps to both encourage clearer, more discernible images, and foster a better understanding of what you're seeing. More experienced practitioners can even scry regarding a certain person, situation, or scenario.

If you're the energetic type and patience is not your forte, scrying may not be the type of divination that works for you. Luckily, there are many other methods out there if scrying just isn't your thing.

This type of divination is helpful in bringing forth subconscious thoughts, solutions to problems, obstacles, and clarity to situations. Scrying can be a handy tool to use when looking to enhance your manifestation as it may bring forth some aspects that you hadn't thought to address or potential obstacles that are hindering your manifestation.

8

YOUR STATE OF MIND AND SELF-CARE—GLOW UP FOR GREATNESS

You've probably heard the saying "happiness is a state of mind." While this certainly isn't always the case, it has long been proven that your state of mind is immensely powerful. It is also paramount to successful manifestation. In this chapter, you'll discover exactly how powerful your state of mind is, how it relates to manifestation, and you'll learn ways that you can nurture and maintain it to more easily manifest your way into the life of your dreams.

HOW YOUR STATE OF MIND CAN CHANGE YOUR LIFE

Have you ever had a day when you woke up on the wrong side of the bed and after the first negative thing happens, it just turns from a bad morning into a bad day? Most of us have wondered why bad things tend to cascade in this way, and now we are beginning to understand that your state of mind can be a large part of it.

To begin with, your state of mind can affect your relationships, your career, and even your physical health. If we explore it further, it becomes a little more clear why. If you have a negative state of mind, this often transfers into being snappy, irritable, and more sensitive, which in turn, can easily lead to conflict and arguments (which will negatively impact your state of mind even more.)

If we explore the effects of a negative state of mind on your career, aside from being less effective in the collaborative sense for the above reasons, your concentration will be impaired, you will be less likely to listen with an open mind, and you may even miss opportunities to improve your position. One global research initiative even found that "Calm, Happy and Energized" states of mind are the three that drive the greatest levels of effectiveness and performance within organizations (Caillet, Hirshberg, & Stefano Petti, 2014).

Lastly, your health is intrinsically linked to your state of mind. This is because of something called the "mind-body connection." This connection means that negative emotions cause signals in your brain to release chemicals and hormones that affect your body in certain ways. The most familiar and common of these chemicals being cortisol, affectionately nicknamed the "stress hormone." In a fight-or-flight situation, this hormone is very useful in getting us out of a bind, but the long-term effects of high levels of cortisol leads to poor health in the form of cardiovascular disease, digestive disorders, infection, and more.

As I'm sure you've also noticed, this ties in directly with the first law of attraction "like attracts like." The more negative your mindset, the worse off your day (or month) will be. The good news is that you have the power to change that, and the benefits are limitless.

Some of the benefits that you can enjoy from nurturing a good state of mind include:

- Better health and less likelihood to develop chronic conditions
- Greater resilience against disease
- Longer lifespan
- Improved ability to make decisions and solve problems
- Lower stress and less likelihood to develop mental illness
- Higher likelihood to recognize (and seize) opportunities
- Improved coping skills during times of stress
- Improved ability to deal with and express emotions in an appropriate way
- Greater intrinsic happiness and ability to enjoy activities
- Increased engagement
- Improved performance (at work and in creative pursuits)

Nurturing a positive state of mind will help you to get out of the habit of negative thinking and negative self-talk that has become so prevalent in our society. It has even been known to improve mental illness (I am proof of this.)

The best way to manifest effectively is to try to nurture a positive state of mind, and self-care is a great way to do that.

WHAT IS SELF-CARE?

Self-care, as the phrase suggests, is about caring for yourself. More than that, it is about nurturing and sustaining a positive mindset and trying to meet your needs, mental, physical, and spiritual.

Most of what you see about self-care is lighting a candle and having a bubble bath. While this is a perfectly acceptable action of self-care, this is not always what this is about. For proper self-care, you need to first understand and list the things that you actually need. A good way to do this is usually to see where your negative thoughts come from and what kind of thoughts or situations cause you to have a negative mindset.

For example, if you find that you feel stressed and overwhelmed because you never seem to have any time to yourself, that is a need that isn't being met that you would need to address with self-care. In this case, you may need to carve out 15 minutes of your day to do something you enjoy, like a bubble bath, if that's what you like, but this can also be reading, watching TV, doing a hobby, talking to a friend, or simply just sitting quietly and breathing.

The important thing about this is that you need to identify *all* of the needs that currently aren't being met. Self-care is about balance, so just addressing one need that isn't being met with a 15-minute time-out every so often (or daily) isn't going to bring about any major changes in your mindset.

This also means that self-care isn't always doing things that are indulgent. As much as we'd like for self-care to only entail eating chocolates, drinking wine, and having bubble baths while listening to our favorite music, self-care can sometimes be difficult and will challenge us to do activities that are right for us, rather than just doing what is easy or feels good.

For example, if you find that you are stressed out about money because you have important expenses that you are struggling to pay, that is a need that isn't currently being met and would need to be addressed with self-care. This particular self-care would look more like budgeting, assessing if there's a route to a raise or promotion and what work that would entail, potentially updating your CV and applying for a better paying job, and actively looking for ways to cut your expenses. This will be a challenging exercise that will take time and effort.

As difficult as it may be to do these kinds of self-help exercises that are less about indulgence and are more about discipline, you will find that even working towards meeting your needs will put you in a more positive mindset and will give you more confidence. Taking control of your happiness by working towards goals that will benefit you is in itself a very positive self-help (and manifestation) technique.

This applies to every part of your life, including your emotional and spiritual needs. The key to a positive mindset is to try and foster balance in your life so that you can work towards all your needs simultaneously, and not leave any part of you neglected.

As you're probably realizing by now, self-care can be a lot of work, and it may also take up a lot of time, but the payoff is that if you are working every day even in a small way to meet all your needs and take care of yourself, all the time and work will be worth it.

Nobody is perfect, so if you find that you occasionally neglect your self-care by overworking on a particular day, or sleeping late, or missing the gym, it's ok! The idea behind self-care is that it should be working towards making you feel good, so if a temporary break from one or more of those activities is what you need to feel good, then do it!

Ultimately, your self-care activities should also complement each other. If, for example, you suffer from confidence issues because of your weight and part of your self-care to address this is exercise, but you also suffer with emotional issues and a lack of discipline or resilience, you will find that working on your emotional and mental issues with discipline and resilience will in turn help you to keep up with your exercise.

WAYS THAT YOU CAN PRACTICE SELF-CARE

So now that you understand what self-care is, here are some examples of self-care activities that you can do for common needs that many people aren't meeting:

Get Enough Quality Sleep

This is one that probably has you rolling your eyes with a giant 'duh!'. However, most people aren't getting enough good quality sleep (and are even aware of this.) In fact, 62% of adults around the world say they don't sleep as well as they'd like, and worse, 80% want to improve their sleep, but 60% of them have not sought help (Philips Global Sleep Survey, 2019).

Sleep is a very important activity that we all need more than we think. It helps us stay healthy by giving us the time our bodies need to repair, which helps us stave off disease and keeps our brain in tip top function (as coffee junkies would know, without sufficient sleep, your brain can't function properly.)

This self-care can look like:

- Creating a proper sleep schedule by attempting to go to bed at the same time every day and waking up at the same time.
- Ensuring you get at least 8 hours every night (I myself struggle with this one having two small children, therefore, I try to get to bed by 9 p.m.).
- Not eating anything an hour before bed (this can cause poor quality sleep and heartburn.)
- Keeping distractions like TV, phones, and computers out of the bedroom so you can wind down properly.

- Avoiding sugar and caffeine 3-4 hours before bed (this can keep you up.)
- Ensuring that you have 30 minutes of wind down time before bed that consists of light activities that will calm your mind (like light reading, mediation, yoga, or breathing exercises.)

Eat a Healthy Diet

Another self-care activity that you had probably already guessed, a healthy balanced diet will make a big difference to your life in a whole host of ways. Despite it being common knowledge that a healthy diet is important to maintain your health, just under half of all Americans have a poor diet, and globally 11 million deaths a year are linked to poor diet (Aubrey, 2019).

The truth is you *are* what you eat. A healthy diet can:

- Help you live longer
- Keep you healthy
- Boost your immunity and avoid illness
- Improved brain health and cognitive abilities
- Improved mood
- Sustained energy throughout the day

All these benefits will help you to maintain a healthy and positive state of mind. Some ways that you can practice self-care in this way include:

- Eating fruit and vegetables daily (preferably 5 portions.)
- Limiting your saturated and trans fat and eating more plant-based fats like those found in fish, avocado, olive oil, and nuts.

- Eating enough protein (25%-35% of your daily calories.)
- Try to get enough fiber in your diet per day (around 30g) as this has been shown to maintain a healthy gut and also assists in maintaining your ideal weight.
- Having more complex carbohydrates (like oats, brown and wild rice, rye and wholewheat breads), than refined carbohydrates (like white bread, white rice, etc.) as this assists with sustained energy, balanced blood sugar levels, and more fiber intake, which keeps you regular and your gut healthy.
- Drink at least 8 glasses of water a day (more if you are exercising.)
- Limiting your intake of processed food, sugar, salt, and junk food.

Exercise

This is another common self-care activity that may seem obvious, but many people struggle to find the time to fit it in when they have busy schedules. The truth is that even a little bit of exercise or activity that gets your body moving makes a huge difference to your health and wellbeing.

I myself aim for 10,000 steps each day. It can be a motivating factor if you are nearly at your 10k goal to just do 10 minutes of stepping (maybe to a YouTube video) to get you over that hurdle.

Some benefits of regular exercise include:

- Increased health
- Boosted immunity; helps prevent you from getting sick
- Better sustained energy throughout the day

- Improved mood and increased endorphins
- Controls your weight
- Promotes better sleep
- Can assist socially if it's a group activity

All these benefits will go a long way towards promoting a positive state of mind and even assists with other self-care activities like sleep, weight, and emotional regulation (from improved mood.) Some ways that you can practice this kind of self-care are:

- Try an activity that can double as a hobby like sports or dancing.
- Try to get active for at least 30 minutes per day.
- Do an activity that you enjoy; there's no reason your exercise has to be unpleasant.
- Try to get in walks wherever you can; they can be social and they can be helpful in winding down or thinking a matter over.
- If you like the outdoors, things like hiking and trail biking can combine the positive effects of nature and the benefits of exercise into one. My personal favorite location is the beach so I can listen to the soothing sounds of the ocean.
- Try wherever you can to fit in exercise in your day; that is, take the stairs instead of the elevator, park further away, carry your groceries in a basket rather than a cart, and walk rather than drive where possible.

Reframe Your Thinking

The self-care thus far has been mostly physical, but this one is more about your mental state and way of thinking.

This is a self-care exercise that you can use to challenge your bias towards negativity and negative self-talk (which is very common for many people.) The first step in this is to be able to identify negative or damaging thoughts when they arise. Things to look out for include:

- Magnifying - making matters seem bigger or worse than they are.
- Polarizing - seeing things as black or white, with no gray or inbetween (things are either good or bad).
- Catastrophizing - making assumptions that the worst scenario will happen when there's no reasonable reason to think so.
- Filtering - you only focus on the negative things that happened to you and ignore the positive.
- Blaming - you don't take responsibility for things that are your fault and rather blame everyone else.
- Personalizing - you make everything about you and assume that everything negative is either aimed in your direction or your fault.
- Perfectionism - comparing yourself to an impossible and imaginary perfect ideal and setting yourself up for failure.
- "Shoulda, woulda, coulda" - this is when you obsess over the things that you should've or could've done to prevent or mitigate a bad situation or event.

When these thinking patterns or thoughts occur, it's good practice to learn to identify them. Once you have identified them, you can begin to stop yourself when these thoughts arise and change your narrative and way of thinking. Some ways to do this include:

- Start practicing gratitude and looking for the positive things in your life daily; you'll start seeing more to be grateful about after doing this for a while. Remember the gratitude journal we talked about? This is one of my daily must-haves!
- Identify situations that consistently upset you that need to change. If you're finding that a friendship/relationship, your commute, or a part of your job makes you unhappy, find ways to slowly change these things (talking to the friend/partner, taking a different route/method of transport, doing things differently at work.)
- Try to catch your negative thoughts and transform them into more positive ones. "I've had a bad day" can be changed to, "I will have a much better day tomorrow." You don't need to pretend to be happy all the time, but don't dwell on the negative longer than necessary.
- Talk to yourself with kindness and catch yourself when you start speaking badly to yourself. Instead of "I'm so stupid," you can say, "I'm really struggling to understand this, but everyone struggles and this is normal." Remember to ask yourself if you would talk to a friend this way. You need to start talking to yourself the way you do to other people that you love. Self love starts here.
- Remember to laugh; all situations, even bad ones, may have an element of humor to them. The more you laugh at yourself and even at some of your problems, the less heavy and serious they will feel. Laughter is so powerful that it has even been suggested to be a form of medicine.

Look Good to Feel Good

How do you feel when you haven't showered, brushed your teeth, or your hair looks like a mess? I'm going to guess that you would at least feel self-conscious if not actively uncomfortable and bad about yourself. When we feel that we look good, that we smell good, then we tend to feel better. Sometimes, when you've had a bad day and you take a shower, how many times have you felt better once you were clean and dressed in clean clothes?

It's also another small way that we can take control of our lives and, in some cases, feel pampered. For some ladies, getting their hair or nails done not only makes them feel good afterwards, but makes them feel pampered and special while they are getting it done.

This also goes for our environment. We tend to not feel comfortable in environments that are dirty, untidy, or chaotic either.

Some ways that you can do this include:

- Shower or bath daily.
- Brush your teeth daily (aim for at least twice a day.)
- Address any body or breath odor issues by changing your products or speaking with your doctor/dentist.
- Ensure your hair is tidy and well kept (if you have it colored, keep up with it, keep it trimmed and brushed; don't let it have too much overgrowth, split ends, or get tangled and wild.) If you enjoy getting it done at the salon, make the time to do so.
- Ensure your nails are tidy. If you like having your nails done at a salon, make the time to do so.

- Ensure that you wear clean clothes daily.
- Try to keep up with the washing enough to ensure clean clothes daily.
- Try to keep your house hygienically clean if not always completely tidy; remember you can outsource these tasks! You don't have to do it all; if you have a significant other or roommate, ask them to assist, or even consider getting a cleaning service if you need the extra help.
- Make your bed every day.
- Keep the dishes from piling up in the sink.
- Try to have a day when you do larger cleans that includes things like the bathrooms, the floors, and dusting.
- Dress in a way that you feel confident and comfortable.

9

THE POWER OF MEDITATION AND AFFIRMATIONS—YES YOU CAN!

If there's two activities you've heard mentioned repeatedly in conjunction with manifestation by now, it's 'meditation' and 'affirmations.' This is because they are very powerful techniques to enhance your manifestations, and in this chapter, you will learn why this is the case.

MEDITATION: MORE THAN JUST CROSS-LEGGED OMS

When you think of meditation, your first thought may be of yoga, or monks sitting cross-legged in temples chanting "om." What do the two scenarios have in common? Mindfulness. This is also what links meditation and manifestation together. Mindfulness is what allows you to slow your thoughts and just exist in the present moment. It allows you not only to empty your mind, but to focus on a specific thought without the distraction of other thoughts or worries.

So, how does this help you in manifestation? To begin with, it helps you with visualization manifestation techniques, as it assists you in accessing your imagination and fully focusing on your goal without intrusive thoughts or worries.

You can also use your manifestation goal as your meditation mantra. In a trance state, this allows your goal and intention to sink into your subconscious mind while also focusing on the goal consciously as you say it. Mantras are repeated words or sounds (like om) that people use during meditation to reach a deeper state of meditation or trance state. When you use your goals or affirmations as a mantra, it can help you maintain a connection to the state that you would like to encourage.

Remember when we spoke about our energy and vibrations? Well, meditation is also an activity that raises our vibration, which is important to facilitate the manifestation of our goals and attract the positive into our lives.

Lastly, meditation helps you to become more in touch with yourself, be more aware when your emotional and mental state is in trouble or in need of attention, and you will become more intuitive. This will allow you to recognize and seize opportunities in addition to having insight into what actions you could be taking to further your goals.

Not only will meditation assist you with your manifestation directly in these ways, but it will also indirectly assist you to manifest through the physical and mental benefits that will improve your state of mind.

Meditation has shown the have the following benefits:

- Raises your vibration (frequency)
- Lowers stress
- Improves sleep quality
- Lowers resting heart rate and blood pressure
- Reduces negative emotions
- Improves mental focus
- Reduces intrusive thoughts and "brain chatter"

- Increases self awareness
- Increases creativity and expands imagination
- Improves ability to handle stress and difficult situations
- Promotes acceptance and joy

An important thing to remember when you start trying to meditate is that, like most things, practice hones it and allows it to be more effective. When you first start meditation, you will find that it might be difficult to quiet your body and/or thoughts; you'll find that your day-to-day thoughts and worries will intrude on your time and you may find yourself getting bored or distracted. Don't panic! All these things are completely normal and will improve with time.

The great thing about meditation is that there are a variety of ways to do it, so if the "sitting cross-legged with your eyes closed" version doesn't work for you, you're bound to find the kind that does.

Below are some examples of different types of meditation that you could explore:

- **Yoga** requires that you focus on your breath, your posture, and how your body feels; this allows you to be truly present in the moment and allows you to practice active mindfulness.
- **Guided meditation** is where you are led on a mental journey by a teacher or guide and are required to visualize and create imagery of this journey or situation, including the sensations that go with it; this can be very effective for manifestation. You can actually try this out right away as there's a link to a free guided meditation for you at the end of this book!

- **Tai Chi** is an ancient Chinese martial art that is gentle on the body and mind as it focuses on deep breathing, slow movements, and holding postures in a gentle, graceful manner, always going at your own pace; like yoga, this helps to practice mindfulness as your mind is emptied of everything but the breathing and motions.
- **Mantra meditation** is a practice where you repeat a sound, word, or phrase repeatedly, allowing you to go into a trance state in addition to drowning out other thoughts or worries.
- **Walking meditation** is when you combine your relaxing walk with meditation, either emptying your mind of all else but the sights and sensations of the walk, or focusing on particular thoughts of manifestation.

MEDITATION TECHNIQUES

So now that you know how powerful meditation is, where do you start? To begin with, find a quiet spot where you know that you won't be disturbed. This can be in your house, on your bed, outside on a picnic blanket or on the grass, or even just on your couch. As long as you are comfortable, the area is as free from distractions as possible, and you can be assured of as much quiet as possible. Ensure that your area is relaxing to you; if you would like to light some incense or a candle or put on some nice soothing music, feel free to do so.

Next, make sure that you are dressed comfortably (in loose clothes if possible) and that you are at a comfortable temperature. If you feel like you might need a jacket or blanket near you during the meditation, bring one to have in reach.

Find a comfortable position in your designated area,

whether that is cross-legged, lying on your back, or your side, on your knees, whatever position is most comfortable and will be sustainable for a long time. If you need a pillow under your head, knees, or between your knees if you're lying on your side, go for it.

Close your eyes and concentrate on your breathing. Breathe slowly, and deeply. If you want to use a breathing pattern, you can do so (a breathing pattern is breathing in for a certain count and breathing out for a certain count.) A common one is square breathing such as breathing in for six counts and out for six counts, or elongating the exhale such as in for six counts and out for eight counts.

Once you are breathing slowly and deeply consistently and don't need to concentrate on it any longer, you can start relaxing your body. Focus on relaxing each body part independently, starting at your head and ending at your toes or vice versa.

If you are looking to do a mediation where you empty your mind, there are a few visualizations that can help you achieve this and let your body reach full relaxation:

- Imagine that your thoughts are dandelions that are being blown away by the wind until your head is empty of thoughts.
- Imagine that you are sinking into the earth.
- Imagine a blank page.
- Imagine a night sky.
- Focus on a sound (like a fan or air conditioner) and let everything else but that specific sound fade away.

These may assist you in quieting your mind and emptying your head of thoughts and mind chatter. It is normal for your mind to wander; simply notice when it happens and return to your breathing.

If you are looking to do a mantra meditation, you can start either saying out loud, or quietly within your mind, the goal or affirmation that you would like to manifest. It is usually easier if your goal or manifestation is as short and to the point as possible. Something like, "I am getting a promotion," or "I'm getting the body I want," or "I'll receive money soon" are easier and more effective to chant than something like, "Through hard work and dedication, I will earn a promotion at work."

If you were hoping to do some visualization during your meditation, you can start to imagine the goal you would like to manifest and how it came to be. Imagine how achieving your goal would feel. If you like, you can imagine what steps that you've taken would lead up to this goal. Hold this in your mind for as long as you can.

When you notice that your mind wanders, and it will, don't be hard on yourself. Examine the thoughts and worries that pop up without judgment, and then let them go. Gently guide your thoughts back to your desired focus or complete another visualization to try to empty your mind.

If you only have a certain amount of time to put towards your meditation practice, set a timer so that you don't have the anxiety that your meditation is taking too long or that you're missing time on other activities you need to get to. This will help to prevent such worries from popping up repeatedly during your meditation practice. When you first start, just aim for 15 minutes per day.

Once you are ready to end your meditation, it can be helpful to bring your attention back to your body first. Wiggle your toes and touch your fingertips together before gently opening your eyes. Give yourself a moment to come back to yourself. If you jump up and get back to normal life, you might find the experience a bit jarring. After opening your eyes, it can be pleasant to stretch your body and/or shake it out. This is a great way to bring yourself back to reality in a gentle and fun way.

If you are looking to meditate regularly, it is usually easier to find a time that works for you daily and fit it into your routine than doing it whenever you "have a moment" or when you feel like it. Sometimes, it takes some time to actually reap the benefits before you actually feel like meditating.

AFFIRMATIONS: HOW DO THEY WORK?

Now we reach the most common tool of manifestation; affirmations. But what are they and how do they work?

Affirmations are positive statements regarding yourself, your abilities, and your goals that help to shift your mindset and outlook to challenge negative thoughts and self-doubt while preventing self-sabotaging behavior. In short, affirmations remind you that you have the ability to achieve your goals.

Affirmations work because our brains sometimes have difficulty distinguishing reality from what we imagine and tell ourselves. So if we keep telling ourselves things like "I can't do this," "I'll never achieve this goal," "I'm so stupid" then our brain starts to believe this and we subconsciously start acting accordingly. Negative self-talk is unfortunately a very common phenomenon, and every time you engage in it, you are actively standing in the way of achieving your goals.

Affirmations have also been shown to engage the same parts of the brain when we visualize ourselves doing something or completing a goal as when we actually do achieve it. So our brains will start to take our words as fact, whether we are talking positively or negatively.

In psychology, affirmations work by enhancing and

supporting your sense of self-integrity. Self-integrity is our perceived power and ability to achieve our goals and resilience against threats to our concept of self. This directly relates to a psychological theory called "self-affirmation theory."

Self-affirmation theory has three main ideas behind why affirmations work. Firstly, affirmations give us a full and ongoing narrative of who we are and what we are capable of. This allows our self-identity to be flexible and adaptable to different circumstances, and with it, our specific ideas on what success is and what successful traits could be according to the situation. This also means that we don't need to hold ourselves to impossible standards in order to consider ourselves successful, but show competence and confidence in activities and situations that we personally value.

Some of the scientifically proven benefits of affirmations include:

- Lowers stress and the deterioration of health associated with it
- Helps us to perceive critical messages with less resistance
- Positively influences academic achievement
- Aids people to increase their physical behavior to achieve their goals
- Encourages people to improve their wellbeing
- Boosts self-esteem
- Aids those with mental illness
- Helps people perform better at work

It's important to note that affirmations will only work if done regularly. Telling yourself something positive once in a while is not going to give you the benefits that you want. It needs to be consistent, and aside from becoming an active daily activity, it also works best as a reaction to negative self-talk and self-doubt. By identifying negative thoughts and replacing them with positive affirmations, you will constantly affirm your value and ability to achieve your goals.

Another important aspect to remember is that you can't just pick an affirmation, such as "I am happy" and then repeat it to yourself consistently when you are miserably unhappy and you know that this isn't true. A part of what makes affirmations work is that you can believe in them. So, instead of choosing an affirmation that you feel isn't true, replace it with something that you can believe in, such as, "I am working through my difficulties with grace," or "I am working hard for the life I deserve." Always look to word your affirmations in a way that you can agree with (but always keep them positive.)

Following on from this, avoid toxic positivity, especially when you are going through a difficult time or are faced with an unpleasant situation. Saying things like "I am fine," "I am unbothered by this situation," or, "I am perfectly happy" invalidates your feelings and won't be statements that you actually believe. Rather, acknowledge the negative emotions that you are feeling, but focus on the positive aspects of how you can deal with it. Affirmations such as, "This situation will pass and I will feel better soon," or "I am actively working to improve this situation," or, "I have the strength and grace to handle this," or simply, "these negative feelings will pass." These types of statements will strengthen your belief that you have the ability to get through the situation and that you will be ok in the future, rather than pressuring you to be ok when you aren't.

AFFIRMATIONS: WHERE TO START

To begin with your affirmations, you must first see what areas of your life you'd like to change and define what your goals are. Sometimes, it's helpful once you've identified what your goals are, what kind of qualities or behavior you would need to meet that goal and incorporate this into your affirmations. For example, if you need to be quick thinking, or have confidence to speak in front of people to achieve your goal, some of your affirmations should be, "I am quick thinking," or, "my speed in thinking on my feet is always improving," or, "I am confident," or, "I am gaining confidence every day." This will help you to cultivate not just your goal, but the traits you will need to achieve it.

When writing your affirmations, write them in the present tense rather than the future tense. This will help to convince your subconscious that you are already prepared and in the process of achieving your goals. If you phrase your goals in the future tense like, "I will get a fulfilling job," your brain will process this as something that you aren't already working on, and it reaffirms to yourself that it is a goal that will only be fulfilled sometime in the future.

Linked to this, your affirmations should also be as specific as possible. While you can have affirmations such as, "I am feeling happier every day," it might be more effective to link your affirmations to specific goals. If you are feeling lonely and your goal is to make more friends or spend more time with your friends, then using affirmations that link directly to those behaviors and feelings will be more effective than general statements that could apply to anyone at any time. Remember that affirmations are all about you!

The next step is to try to put aside feelings of silliness or thoughts that you're being ridiculous. Let's be honest, it can feel weird at first to stare at yourself in a mirror and say nice things repeatedly, but like all things, feeling comfortable with this practice takes time and patience. Give yourself time, and for the first few times, do them in a way that makes you the most comfortable. If you want to start by writing them in a journal or saying them silently during meditation, do that. Then allow yourself to branch out with ways that you are a little less comfortable with.

The last step is just to repeat your affirmations as often as you can. Make them a part of your routine, like when you wake up and before you go to sleep. Like meditation, or any other hobby, you need to consciously make time for your affirmations for them to assist you in manifesting your desires. Start with 3-5 minutes, twice a day. Try to repeat your affirmations at least ten times each. Repetition is key to helping the message sink in.

Below are some examples of affirmations that you can start out with if you are nervous or unsure how to write your own from the get-go:

- My body is healthy and strong.
- I am healing every day and getting stronger.
- I am good at my job.
- I am successful.
- I deserve the raise.
- I am creating my ideal body.
- I am worthy.
- I am resilient.
- I am abundant.
- Money comes easily and frequently.
- I appreciate all that I have.

10

SPELLS FOR BEGINNERS— MANIFESTING YOUR DREAM LIFE

Now that you have the secrets to manifestation magic, get ready to try some manifestation spells to get you started on the path to your dream life. Before performing any of the below spells, revise or keep in mind everything that you learned from the manifestation magic chapter. Keep yourself safe at all times and believe in what you are doing. You are the magic!

SPELLS FOR MONEY

Candle and Bowl Money Spell

What you'll need:

- 1 x green candle
- Oakmoss or Patchouli essential oil
- Agate or aventurine
- A small bowl

- A collection of small stones (more the larger your candle is)
- Optional: sigil for wealth

Method:

1. Rub your candle with the chosen essential oil and attach or decorate your candle with the chosen crystals.
2. If you would like to use a sigil, engrave your sigil for wealth or money on the candle.
3. Place the bowl in front of your candle.
4. Light your candle and place a stone in the small bowl while saying the following incantation:

As the number of stones multiples, may my money grow.
As this anointed candle burns, let my wealth overflow.
I remove all blocks to hamper my success.
Open all opportunities and goals to progress.
As I say it , so it will be.
So mote it be.

5. Burn the candle every day for three or nine minutes and place a stone in the bowl every time you do so.
6. Remember to practice gratitude when you receive the desired outcome.

Money Spell Jar/Pouch

What you'll need:

- Green pouch OR glass jar/bottle with lid or cork
- Dried Dill
- Dried Fennel

MANIFESTING MAGIC

- Agate and/or Topaz
- Bergamot/Patchouli essential oil
- Sage incense or smudge stick
- Green candle and lighter if using a bottle/jar
- Optional: rune or sigil for money/wealth/success
- Optional: Paper with specific amount on it (if you just generally want to boost your wealth you can leave this out, but if you want a particular amount, write it down on a piece of paper)

Method:

1. Light your sage incense or smudge stick and either place the smoking end in the bottle/jar until it has filled with smoke or let the pouch pass through the smoke (this is the cleansing step).
2. Fill the bottle with the dried herbs, the crystals and the essential oil one by one; as you do so, hold in your mind an image of you receiving money, of your bank account increasing, or of ways that your wealth will increase.
3. If you have a specific amount in mind, place the paper with the amount on it inside the bottle/pouch, while holding that amount clearly in your mind.
4. If you have a sigil for money/wealth/success or you would like to use a rune, add the piece of paper with the symbol on it into the bottle/pouch while once again imagining your wealth increasing or the method in which you'd like for this to occur.
5. If you have used a bottle or a jar, close the lid or put the cork in it and seal it by melting the green candle wax over the lid/cork until it is completely sealed.
6. If you have a pouch, pull it closed.
7. Keep this money jar/pouch in your handbag, or on

your desk at work; just keep it close to you where you can touch it or look at regularly
8. Everytime you see or handle it, remember that it is actively working towards your goal.

SPELLS FOR PROTECTION

Protection Talisman Spell

What you'll need:

- A piece of jewelry that you/intended recipient wears all the time OR if they don't currently wear jewelry and enjoy crystal jewelry, a necklace, ring, bracelet with one of the following crystals: Jet, Jasper, Obsidian, Onyx, Tiger's Eye
- Clove or sandalwood incense
- Jasmine flowers
- Black candle
- Moon water (water charged under the full moon)
- If the jewelry does not contain any crystals, one crystal of any of the following: Jet/Jasper/Obsidian/Onyx/Tiger's Eye
- Optional: Sigil for protection if you have one or rune for protection if you use them

Method:

1. The best day to do this spell is a Tuesday.
2. If possible, place the gems in the North direction, the incense in the East direction, the candle in the South direction, and the water in the West direction; you can either use a compass to determine what direc-

tions these would be or simply put them around yourself in the same way as a compass with the gems in front of you, the candle behind you, the water to your left, and the intense to your right.

3. Take the jewelry and place them on the gems in front of you (if they are made of the gems, simply place them in front of you) and say, "Elements of Earth, grant the bearer of this talisman protection."

4. Take the jewelry and turn to your right and wave the incense over your jewelry, pushing it through the smoke and say, "Elements of Air, grant the bearer of this talisman protection."

5. Take the jewelry and turn to the candle behind you and pass the jewelry (quickly and carefully not to damage it) through the flame of the candle and say, "Element of Fire, grant the bearer of this talisman protection."

6. Take the jewelry and turn to your left and either dip the the jewelry in the water, or if it could be damaged by water, dip your fingers in the moon water and flick it gently at the jewelry without actually wetting it too much and say, "Element of Water, grant the bearer of this talisman protection."

7. Finally, hold the talisman, close your eyes, and imagine the wearer of the jewelry enclosed in a bubble of protection or forcefield (optional: you can say "(Spirits/Deity of your choice), grant the bearer of this talisman protection".)

Protection Candle Spell

What you'll need:

- Black candle
- Clove or sandalwood essential oil
- Dried rosemary
- Obsidian/Jet and tiger's eye
- Optional: Protection sigil or protective rune
- Lighter

Method:

1. Anoint or rub the essential oil over the candle.
2. Optional: carve the protection rune/sigil onto the candle.
3. Roll the candle in or otherwise sprinkle the rosemary over the candle.
4. Decorate or attach the crystals onto the candle.
5. Light the candle and recite the incantation:

As the flame burns will all danger and harm be turned away,
All who reside here will be safe throughout the night and day.
Banish all living and dead with ill intent.
Through the burning of this candle, seal our safety for all events.
So I say it, so shall it be.
So mote it be (x 3).

SPELLS FOR JOBS AND YOUR CAREER

Manifestation Box to Get a Job

Things that you'll need:

- An 8-inch long rectangular box (can be a wooden box, a glass box, a jewelry box)
- Carnelian
- Chrysoprase
- Tourmaline
- Cinnamon
- Comfrey
- Bay leaf
- Bergamot incense/essential oil
- Sage incense
- Optional: Sigil for getting a job
- If you know what companies you'd like to work at or the jobs you want, you can bring the job advert or the business card/s of the companies.

Method:

1. Light the sage incense and let the smoke fill up the box (cleansing step.)
2. Fill the box with the crystals, the herbs, and the essential oil if you used one, while imagining your dream job coming closer to you (if you used an incense instead of an essential oil, light it and let the smoke fill the box.)
3. Carve your sigil on/in your box or draw it on a piece of paper and put it in the box.
4. If you have the printed job adverts or business

cards of the companies you want to work at, drop them into the box and imagine yourself receiving an email or call from them confirming your position there.
5. Keep your manifestation box near your computer or where you sit most of the time. and if you find additional jobs or business cards, feel free to add them.
6. Every time you look at the box, know that it is working toward your intent.

Spell to Grow Your Career

What you'll need:

- A pot of soil
- Alfalfa seeds
- A label for the pot
- Cinnamon
- Bergamot/Sandalwood incense
- Carnelian
- Chrysoprase
- Tourmaline
- Water in a watering can

Method:

1. Write your position or simply, "My Career" on the label and put it on the pot of soil.
2. Shake some cinnamon over the soil and plant the alfalfa seeds while imagining your career advancing and growing.
3. Decorate your pot with the crystals while holding in your mind the success you want to manifest for your career.

4. Light an incense stick and push it into soil while still imagining the growth of your career.

5. Water your seeds gently and say,

As these seeds grow and flourish, so will my career.
For every challenge that is laid before me, I will persevere.
As these plants take root, so shall my ambition.
All my hopes for my career will come to their fruition.
So I say it, so shall it be.
So mote it be (x 3).

6. Water and nurture your seeds and resulting plants with care.

SPELLS FOR LOVE AND RELATIONSHIPS

Spell Bag to Attract Love

Things you will need:

- Rose quartz
- Topaz
- Lapis Lazuli
- Dried apple
- Rose petals (dried or fresh)
- Jasmine flowers (dried or fresh)
- Ylang-ylang essential oil or incense
- Optional: Sigil or rune for love on a piece of paper

Method:

1. Drop your essential oil onto your bag or pass the bag through the incense smoke.

2. Add the flower petals, the dried apple, and the crystals into the bag while imagining the type of person and relationship that you would like to attract with each addition.

3. Add the piece of paper with the sigil/rune and continue to hold the person or relationship that you would like to attract in your mind.

4. Keep your spell bag on you at all times, especially when there is a high chance of meeting new people.

Spell For Strengthening Your Relationship

Things you will need:

- Two bottles (glass or plastic); one glass and one plastic is also fine
- Rose quartz
- Topaz
- Lapis Lazuli
- 2 sets of small labels; you can pre-print these if you want it to be pretty
- 2 sets of large labels; you can pre-print these if you want it to be pretty
- Moon water (or regular water will be fine if you haven't charged any)
- Rose petals (dried)
- Jasmine flowers (dried)
- Yarrow flowers
- Ylang-ylang essential oil
- Optional: Sigil or rune for love or committed relationship on a piece of paper
- Optional: Picture of you and your partner

Method:

1. Think about all the words that you'd like to use to describe your relationship and write or print those on the small labels.
2. Think about all the things that could use some work or attention in your relationship currently and write or print those on another set of the small labels.
3. On the large labels, write or print, "Current Relationship" and "Strengthened Relationship."
4. Label one of your bottles with one of the large labels and the other bottle with the other.
5. Stick all the labels of things that need to be worked on on your "Current Relationship" bottle.
6. Stick all the labels of words that you'd like to use to describe your relationship on your "Strengthened Relationship" bottle and imagine how each word would manifest and how your relationship would grow and change.
7. Decorate your "Strengthened Relationship" bottle with your crystals and hold in your mind how you would like your relationship to grow and the positive feelings that would bring to you both.
8. Drop the dried petals into your "Strengthened Relationship" bottle and continue to hold the image of your strengthened relationship in your mind.
9. If you want to use a picture of you as a couple, stick that to your "Strengthened Relationship" bottle so that you can see the image clearly.
10. Take your moon water (or regular water) and fill the "Current Relationship" bottle while thinking of all the things that you'd like to work on and improve.
11. Take your "Current Relationship" bottle and slowly pour your water from it into the "Strengthened

Relationship" bottle while imagining how your relationship will grow and change to improve your bond and happiness.

12. Add a few drops of essential oil while you continue to hold the image in your mind.

13. Remove the labels on your "Current Relationship" bottle or throw the bottle away.

14. Keep your "Strengthened Relationship" bottle somewhere that is meaningful to you and where you will be able to see it regularly.

SPELLS FOR HEALTH AND HEALING

Poppet For Healing

What you'll need:

- White muslin cloth
- Lemon Balm
- Feverfew
- Chamomile
- String or thread and needle
- Turquoise
- Amber
- Bloodstone
- Optional: taglock, an item that links doll with person (picture/lock of hair etc)

Method:

1. Create a person-shaped doll using the white muslin cloth, string/thread and needle and stuffing it with the herbs; if you are using a taglock, you can either sew it

into the inside of the doll, or if it's a lock of hair, you can stick it to the doll with glue as its own hair.
2. Once your doll is person-shaped, you can either draw or sew eyes, nose, and mouth onto the doll to give it a face; if you are skilled with a needle and thread, you can sew the crystals or buttons as their eyes.
3. Create a small necklace and sew/attach the crystals around the neck of the doll.
4. As you create the doll, hold the person in your mind and imagine them getting better; think about the particular ailment you want to heal leaving them or disappearing
5. Optional: You can say the following:

Let the herbs and stones of the earth provide healing.
Remove the pain, infection, and bad feeling.
Strengthen the body and the mind.
Leave only peace, good health and joy to find.
With harm to none, my will is done.

6. You can either keep the poppet if you would like to send energy its way until the person is healthy, or you can bury the poppet in the soil the same day as the ritual.

Healing Candle Spell

What you'll need:

- Green candle
- Lemon Balm
- Feverfew
- Chamomile

- Turquoise
- Amber
- Bloodstone
- Eucalyptus essential oil
- Optional: healing sigil or rune
- Optional: picture of the person you want to heal

Method:

1. Anoint/rub the candle with essential oil.
2. If you're using a sigil/rune, carve it into the candle.
3. Roll or sprinkle the herbs all over the candle.
4. Decorate/attach the crystals to the candle.
5. If you want to use a picture of the person you want to heal, prop it up near the candle (but not near enough that it can get damaged).
6. Light the candle and imagine the ailment/illness leaving the person's body and getting well again.

Optional:

Let the herbs and stones of the earth provide healing.
Remove the pain, infection, and bad feeling.
Strengthen the body and the mind.
Leave only peace, good health and joy to find.
With harm to none, my will is done.

7. Burn the candle every day for eight minutes until the candle has burnt out completely.

10 POINTS TO GRYFFINDOR

That was quite some journey, wasn't it? As you have now learned, manifestation and magic go together like peanut butter and jelly, and you already have all you need to use them to create the life that you've always wanted.

Sometimes, life can get a little overwhelming and it may seem like only the strongest fantasy magic from the teeth of dragons and the hair of unicorns will change it. When you feel this way, be patient and trust yourself to be the hero that you really are. You have more control in your life than you think; all you need is a little time, a chunk of patience, a heap of intent, and all the strength of your belief.

If you don't understand everything in this guide on the first read, don't worry, we'll be waiting to go through this with you all over again whenever you need to. We believe in you!

If you've enjoyed the wild ride with us and want more, please give us a good review so we can create more guides like this and provide you with even more information and enlightenment that you'll need on the road to your dream life. May the odds ever be in your favor, may the force be with you, and don't let the muggles get you down.

GLOSSARY

Affirmations: Positive statements regarding yourself, your abilities, and your goals that help to shift your mindset and outlook to challenge negative thoughts and self-doubt while preventing self-sabotaging behavior.

Divination: A form of magic that serves for practitioners to gain insight or guidance for specific situations.

Energetic Frequencies: The speed of your personal vibrations and that of the world around you with higher (faster) vibrations attracting positive things, and lower (slower) vibrations attracting negative things.

Magic: A way of influencing the world or the outcomes of situations through the application of your will supported by the energy of the natural and spiritual world.

Magical Correspondences: Refers to items that "go together" and attract certain energies.

GLOSSARY

Manifestation: A method of creating or manifesting the things you desire through directed will, intent, and personal energy.

Scrying: A form of divination magic where one looks into an opaque or reflective surface to gain insight from one's subconscious (using a crystal ball, for example.)

Self-Care: The activities that you perform to keep your mind, body, and spirit in good health.

Spells: Magical rituals or activities that use your personal energy, will, and intent, and sometimes the energy of spirits and deities, to create a specific outcome.

Tarot Reading: A form of cartomancy (card divination), whereby the practitioner uses a pack of tarot cards to divine insight into the past, present situations, or the future by asking a question and then drawing cards in a certain spread to gain insight from them.

REFERENCES

Adler. (2006). Drawing Down The Moon Witches, Druids, Goddess Worshippers and Other Pagans in America Today. Penguin Compass.

Alexander. (2021). *Do Positive Affirmations Work? What Experts Say*. Cleveland Clinic. https://health.clevelandclinic.org/do-positive-affirmations-work/

Aubrey. (2019). *Bad Diets Are Responsible For More Deaths Than Smoking, Global Study Finds*. NPR. https://www.npr.org/sections/thesalt/2019/04/03/709507504/bad-diets-are-responsible-for-more-deaths-than-smoking-global-study-finds

Brown. (Unknown). *7 Powerful Reasons Why Self-Care is Not Selfish*. Manifest Everyday. https://manifesteveryday.com/self-care-is-not-selfish/

Buckland. (2001). Scottish Witchcraft: The History & Magic of the Picts. Llewellyn Publications.

Burke. (2007). *The New Complete Book of Tarot*. Connections Book Publishing Limited.

Caillet, Hirshberg & Petti. (2014). *How Your State of Mind Affects Your Performance*. Harvard Business Review. https://hbr.org/2014/12/how-your-state-of-mind-affects-your-performance

Carr-Gomm. (2019). What is Druidry?. Druidry.org. https://druidry.org/druid-way/what-druidry

Cunningham. (2007). *Wicca A Guide For The Solitary Practitioner*. (1). Llewellyn Publications.

REFERENCES

Davis. (2018). *Self-Care: 12 Ways to Take Better Care of Yourself*. Psychology Today. https://www.psychologytoday.com/us/blog/click-here-happiness/201812/self-care-12-ways-take-better-care-yourself

Davis. (Unknown). *Manifestation: Definition, Meaning, and How to Do It*. Berkeley Well-being Institute. https://www.berkeleywellbeing.com/manifestation.html

Dugan. (2007). *Natural Witchery*. (1). Llewellyn Publications.

Eliade. (Unknown). Shamanism. Britannica. https://www.britannica.com/topic/shamanism

Estrada. (2019). *What It Actually Means to Raise Your Vibrational Energy—Plus 12 Ways to Do It*. Well + Good. https://www.wellandgood.com/vibrational-energy/

Fischer. (2022). *How to meditate: The beginner's guide to building a meditation habit and practicing mindfulness*. Insider. https://www.insider.com/how-to-meditate

Gelles. (Unknown). *How to Meditate*. New York Times. https://www.nytimes.com/guides/well/how-to-meditate

Greer. (2005). *Encyclopedia of Natural Magic*. (1). Llewellyn Publications.

Guiley. (1999). Witches, Witchcraft & Wicca. (Third Edition) Checkmark Books Infobase Publishing.

Gunter. (Unknown). *How To Master Law Of Attraction Manifestation Meditation*. The Law Of Attraction. https://www.thelawofattraction.com/law-of-attraction-manifestation-meditation/

Habeck. (2020). *25 Manifestation Techniques That Will Help You Conquer Your Goals*. Holly Habeck. https://hollyhabeck.com/2021/01/03/manifestation-techniques/

Hunt. (2018). *The Hippies Were Right: It's All about Vibrations, Man!*. Scientific American. https://blogs.scientificamerican.com/observations/the-hippies-were-right-its-all-about-vibrations-man/

REFERENCES

Kaplan. (2017). *Meditation for Manifesting Your Dreams - And Accomplishing Your Goals*. Forbes. https://www.forbes.com/sites/dinakaplan/2017/04/30/meditation-for-manifesting-your-dreams-and-accomplishing-your-goals/?sh=11ea6db036c2

Lawson. (Unknown). *How Do Thoughts and Emotions Affect Health?*. University of Minnesota. https://www.takingcharge.csh.umn.edu/how-do-thoughts-and-emotions-affect-health

Leotti, Iyengar & Ochsner. (2010). Born to choose: the origins and value of the need for control. *Trends in cognitive sciences*, 14(10), 457–463. https://www.ncbi.nlm.nih.gov/pmc/articles/PMC2944661/

Marley. (Unknown). *State of Mind: Mental wellness can affect every aspect of a person's life*. Community Health Magazine.https://www.communityhealthmagazine.com/health_content_services_network/state-of-mind-mental-wellness-can-affect-every-aspect-of-a-persons-life/article_f1a5cc0b-3d8d-535a-a858-d6da15e24f3d.html#:~:text=Mental%20health%20affects%20every%20dimension,Professor%20of%20Psychology%20Dean%20McKay.

Mayo Clinic Staff. (2022). *Are you getting too much protein?*. Mayo Clinic. https://www.mayoclinichealthsystem.org/hometown-health/speaking-of-health/are-you-getting-too-much-protein#:~:text=How%20much%20protein%20do%20you,per%20kilogram%20of%20body%20weight

Mayo Clinic Staff. (Unknown). Exercise: 7 benefits of regular physical activity. Mayo Clinic. https://www.mayoclinic.org/healthy-lifestyle/fitness/in-depth/exercise/art-20048389

Mayo Clinic Staff. (Unknown). *Meditation: A simple, fast way to reduce stress*. Mayo Clinic. https://www.mayoclinic.org/tests-procedures/meditation/in-depth/meditation/art-20045858

Mayo Clinic Staff. (Unknown). *Positive thinking: Stop negative self-talk to reduce stress*. Mayo Clinic. https://www.mayoclinic.org/healthy-lifestyle/stress-management/in-depth/positive-thinking/art-20043950

Melton. (Unknown). Wicca. Britannica. https://www.britannica.com/topic/Wicca

REFERENCES

Mental Health America Staff. (Unknown). *Taking Good Care Of Yourself*. Mental Health America. https://www.mhanational.org/taking-good-care-yourself

Mind Tools Team. (Unknown). *Using Affirmations Harnessing Positive Thinking*. Mind Tools. https://www.mindtools.com/pages/article/affirmations.htm

Moore. (2019). *Positive Daily Affirmations: Is There Science Behind It?*. Positive Psychology. https://positivepsychology.com/daily-affirmations/

Morgan. (2003). *The Wicca Handbook*. Vega.

Morter. (Unknown). *Energy Medicine: Managing Your Energetic Environment to Master Your Life*. Corporate Wellness Magazine. https://www.corporatewellnessmagazine.com/article/energy-medicine-managing-energetic-environment-master-life

Murmu, Pramanik. (July 2018). Shamanistic Beliefs and Practices: Emerging Trends towards a New Horizon, ResearchGate, 39-44. https://www.researchgate.net/publication/335839879_Shamanistic_Beliefs_and_Practices_Emerging_Trends_towards_a_New_Horizon

Raypole. (2020). *Positive Affirmations: Too Good to Be True?*. Healthline. https://www.healthline.com/health/mental-health/do-affirmations-work#making-them-effective

Regan. (2021). *What Is The Law Of Attraction & How Does It Work?*. Mbg Mindfulness. https://www.mindbodygreen.com/articles/the-law-of-attraction-simplified-what-it-is-and-how-to-use-it/

Rich. (2022). *Mind/Body Connection: How Your Emotions Affect Your Health*. Family Doctor.org. https://familydoctor.org/mindbody-connection-how-your-emotions-affect-your-health/

Sabin. (2006). *Wicca For Beginners*. (1). Llewellyn Publications.

REFERENCES

Scott. (2020). What Is the Law of Attraction?. Very well mind. https://www.verywellmind.com/understanding-and-using-the-law-of-attraction-3144808

SingleCare Team. (2022). *Sleep statistics 2022*. Single Care. https://www.singlecare.com/blog/news/sleep-statistics/#:~:text=62%25%20of%20adults%20around%20the,Global%20Sleep%20Survey%2C%202019).

Stanborough. (2020). *What Is Vibrational Energy?*. Healthline. https://www.healthline.com/health/vibrational-energy

University of Cambridge. (2014). *Feeling powerless increases the weight of the world ... literally*. Science Daily. https://www.sciencedaily.com/releases/2014/02/140203191735.htm

Unknown. (2018). Neopaganism. Encylopedia.com. https://www.encyclopedia.com/philosophy-and-religion/other-religious-beliefs-and-general-terms/miscellaneous-religion/neopaganism

Unknown. (2018). Wicca. History. https://www.history.com/topics/religion/wicca

Unknown. (2020). Ancient Roots, Historical Challenges. Pluralism.org. https://pluralism.org/ancient-roots-historical-challenges

Unknown. (2020). *How To Make A Sigil || Witchcraft 101*. Arcane Alchemy. http://www.arcane-alchemy.com/blog/2020/3/25/how-to-make-a-sigil-witchcraft-101

Unknown. (2020). *The 5 Principles Of Manifestation For Beginners*. The Manifestation Collective. https://themanifestationcollective.co/manifestation-for-beginners/

Unknown. (2022). *11 Popular Tarot Spreads for Beginners and Advanced readers*. A Little Spark of Joy. https://www.alittlesparkofjoy.com/easy-tarot-spreads/

REFERENCES

Unknown. (2022). Gardner, Gerald Brousseau. Encyclopedia.com. https://www.encyclopedia.com/religion/encyclopedias-almanacs-transcripts-and-maps/gardner-gerald-brousseau

Unknown. (2022). Shamanism: Neoshamanism. Encyclopedia.com. https://www.encyclopedia.com/environment/encyclopedias-almanacs-transcripts-and-maps/shamanism-neoshamanism

Unknown. (Unknown). Ancient Order of Druids. British Museum. https://www.britishmuseum.org/collection/term/BIOG257405

Unknown. (Unknown). *Energy Work*. Personal Tao. https://personaltao.com/soul-spirit/energy-work/

Unknown. (Unknown). *How to Manifest What You Want: Manifestation Techniques*. Thrive. https://thriveglobal.com/stories/how-to-manifest-what-you-want-manifestation-techniques/

Unknown. (Unknown). *How to Meditate*. Mindful.org. https://www.mindful.org/how-to-meditate/

Unknown. (Unknown). *Manifestation And Meditation – How A Quiet Mind Attracts An Abundant Life*. Modern Day Manifestations. https://moderndaymanifestations.com/manifestation-and-meditation/

Unknown. (Unknown). *Personal Energy*. Energy Is Real. https://energyisreal.com/explore/about-personal-energy/#:~:text=The%20term%20%E2%80%9Cpersonal%20energy%E2%80%9D%20refers,to%20your%20sense%20of%20self.

WHO Staff. (2020). *Healthy diet*. World Health Organization. https://www.who.int/news-room/fact-sheets/detail/healthy-diet

Wooll. (2022). *Think your dreams into being? Think again, but manifestation methods can help*. Better Up. https://www.betterup.com/blog/manifestation-methods

ABOUT THE AUTHOR

Isabella "Bella" James is a busy mother of two little humans as well as her amazing dog and naughty cat. She enjoys spending her time by the ocean and connecting with nature.

Bella is fairly new to magic (in this life at least), but is enjoying her journey and soaking up all that the spirits and the Goddess have to offer.

As promised earlier in the book, you can find the **free resources** created for you at the following link:

https://www.isabella-james.com/manifestlikeawitch
Password: MAGIC

Printed in Dunstable, United Kingdom